William Finch

The Objections of Infidel Historians Against Christianity

Considered in eight sermons preached at the Bampton Lecture at Oxford, in the

year MDCCXCVII

William Finch

The Objections of Infidel Historians Against Christianity
Considered in eight sermons preached at the Bampton Lecture at Oxford, in the year MDCCXCVII

ISBN/EAN: 9783337087883

Printed in Europe, USA, Canada, Australia, Japan

Cover: Foto ©Lupo / pixelio.de

More available books at **www.hansebooks.com**

THE OBJECTIONS

OF

INFIDEL HISTORIANS AND OTHER WRITERS

AGAINST CHRISTIANITY,

CONSIDERED IN

EIGHT SERMONS

PREACHED AT THE

BAMPTON LECTURE AT OXFORD,

IN THE YEAR MDCCXCVII.

TO WHICH IS ADDED,

A SERMON

Preached before the University, on Sunday, Oct. 18, 1795.

By WILLIAM FINCH, LL.D.

RECTOR OF AVINGTON, BERKS, AND OF TACKLEY, OXFORDSHIRE; ONE OF THE CITY LECTURERS AT ST. MARTIN'S, OXFORD; AND LATE FELLOW OF ST. JOHN'S COLLEGE.

OXFORD:

AT THE UNIVERSITY PRESS, FOR THE AUTHOR;
SOLD BY MESSRS. FLETCHER AND CO. AND J. COOKE;
AND BY F. AND C. RIVINGTON, IN ST. PAUL'S CHURCH-YARD;
AND MR. EGERTON, OPPOSITE THE ADMIRALTY,
LONDON.

1797.

TO

LADY JONES,

OF RAMSBURY MANOR,

IN THE COUNTY OF

WILTS:

THESE SERMONS

ARE RESPECTFULLY INSCRIBED,

BY

HER LADYSHIP'S

MOST OBEDIENT AND OBLIGED

HUMBLE SERVANT,

W. FINCH.

EXTRACT

FROM THE

LAST WILL AND TESTAMENT

OF THE LATE

REV. JOHN BAMPTON,

CANON OF SALISBURY.

―― " I give and bequeath my Lands and
" Eſtates to the Chancellor, Maſters, and
" Scholars of the Univerſity of Oxford for
" ever, to have and to hold all and ſingular
" the ſaid Lands or Eſtates upon truſt, and to
" the intents and purpoſes hereinafter men-
" tioned; that is to ſay, I will and appoint
" that the Vice-Chancellor of the Univerſity
" of Oxford for the time being ſhall take and
" receive

"receive all the rents, issues, and profits
"thereof, and (after all taxes, reparations,
"and necessary deductions made) that he
"pay all the remainder to the endowment
"of eight Divinity Lecture Sermons, to be
"established for ever in the said Univer-
"sity, and to be performed in the manner
"following:

"I direct and appoint, that, upon the first
"Tuesday in Easter Term, a Lecturer be
"yearly chosen by the Heads of Colleges
"only, and by no others, in the room ad-
"joining to the Printing-House, between
"the hours of ten in the morning and two
"in the afternoon, to preach eight Divinity
"Lecture Sermons, the year following, at St.
"Mary's in Oxford, between the commence-
"ment of the last month in Lent Term, and
"the end of the third week in Act Term.

"Also I direct and appoint, that the eight
"Divinity Lecture Sermons shall be preached
"upon either of the following subjects—to
"confirm and establish the Christian Faith,
"and

" and to confute all heretics and schismatics
" —upon the divine authority of the Holy
" Scriptures — upon the authority of the
" writings of the primitive Fathers, as to
" the faith and practice of the primitive
" Church —upon the Divinity of our Lord
" and Saviour Jesus Christ—upon the Di-
" vinity of the Holy Ghost—upon the Ar-
" ticles of the Christian Faith, as compre-
" hended in the Apostles' and Nicene
" Creeds.

" Also I direct, that thirty copies of the
" eight Divinity Lecture Sermons shall be
" always printed, within two months after
" they are preached, and one copy shall be
" given to the Chancellor of the University,
" and one copy to the Head of every Col-
" lege, and one copy to the Mayor of the
" city of Oxford, and one copy to be put
" into the Bodleian Library; and the ex-
" pence of printing them shall be paid out
" of the revenue of the Land or Estates given
" for establishing the Divinity Lecture Ser-
" mons; and the Preacher shall not be paid,
" nor

"nor be entitled to the revenue, before they
"are printed.

"Also I direct and appoint, that no per-
"son shall be qualified to preach the Divi-
"nity Lecture Sermons, unless he hath taken
"the Degree of Master of Arts at least, in
"one of the two Universities of Oxford or
"Cambridge; and that the same person
"shall never preach the Divinity Lecture
"Sermons twice."

SERMON I.

2 Tim. iii. 15.

And that from a Child thou hast known the holy Scriptures, which are able to make thee wise unto Salvation; through Faith, which is in Christ Jesus.

SALVATION! that is the effect of wisdom here, to the production of happiness hereafter, affording an excellent rule of conduct, and an infinite reward; of this the Scriptures, and they alone are capable. Writings merely human may thus far vie with them, in that *they* likewise possess the power of making us wise, but not in general unto Salvation. This happens, not from any defect to which history, for instance, as a species of composition, is necessarily liable, but from the almost universal fault of the writers. It were to be wished, saith a certain author [a],

[a] Guy Patin.

that an historian were, if possible, of no party, country, or religion. As to the last, the wish is, in many instances, accomplished, particularly among us of this nation; the most favourite historians *are* of none.—The effect of which is far different from what the before-mentioned author intended, since there is a general confederacy among such writers against it. And is Salvation so unimportant, so undesirable an object, as to warrant such neglect, contempt, and rejection of it? No! Yet the distinction arising from literary eminence is too frequently accompanied with *vanity*; never so much gratified as when it can appear divested of common prejudices, and averse from established opinions. The children of this world, as far as that is concerned, are wiser than the children of light; a life of vice is often one of distress, the acknowledged parent of ingenuity; and should that be engaged in a literary career, it will be no wonder if a vicious imagination should give free course to the effusions of a corrupted heart. Nay, such as are the writers, such the readers also: in a wealthy and luxurious nation, the generality will rather wish that their vices should be nursed and encouraged, than checked and eradicated, that they should be represented not as defects,

defects, but as excellencies. Now among such, immoral and irreligious writings must not only gain a free admittance, but also be highly acceptable and agreeable. Those too who live by *printing* will, as far as it depends upon them, admit only such works as occasion them most employment; such then as coincide with the public taste will best answer this purpose, and that being generally depraved and vitiated, writings of this description will commonly obtain the most rapid sale, and be most frequently edited.

But this is not the case with the Scriptures. The authors succeeding one another at considerable intervals, and relating a somewhat interrupted series of events, from the very creation down to the time in which they wrote, cannot be conceived capable of any joint or preconcerted plan to advance their own interests; or to have had any other design, than such as all good men must cherish and encourage, that of introducing virtue, by means of a purer religion, into more extensive practice, and of thus promoting greater happiness. They had no inducement to screen, or flatter the vices of any: their writings were intended only for the edification of those for whose use they were composed, and to whom they

they were particularly addressed; and though subsequent councils gave them greater publicity by spreading them among all nations, yet this only proves their wisdom, and excellence, that could thus recommend them to all ages and conditions, after the writers themselves had become extinct, and were no more. They lived too at a time when the art of printing was not yet invented, and relied on other means of support than book-making; a profession now so extensive, yet when abused so dangerous, especially to the interests of virtue and religion. The study of history then is able to make us wise; and since there is no event entirely different from all that ever before happened, it records such facts as will in a great degree be sure, at future periods, to be repeated: their consequences therefore in the former instances will enable us to prognosticate what they will be in the latter; and as the best part of wisdom is constituted by experience, so the study of history renders us wise by encreasing it. But if that of a particular country produces such an effect, much more does that of the world in general. Scarcely a new opinion or practice becomes prevalent in one nation, but it excites imitators in another. Now he that has such general

neral knowledge, derived from this source, will be as much superior to him who is deficient in it, as the extensive *traveller* is to him, who has been all his life confined at home. Nay remarkable events, wherever they happen, have the same effect on contiguous countries, as a pebble thrown into the water: the at first narrow circle expands itself more and more over the surface, and at last reaches its utmost limits. What an opportunity then does the study of general history afford of acquainting ourselves with those conspicuous facts which have illustrated the annals of the world! How enriched the understanding that is abundantly stored with the knowledge of them! How delighted the attention that is frequently employed in meditating upon them! For if to have an intimate acquaintance with the phænomena of nature is highly agreeable, much more so is it to have a clear comprehension of those events which gave rise to kingdoms and empires, or accelerated their fall; which influenced the founder of a state, or weighed with the legislator; which established the reputation of the conqueror, or precipitated the ruin of his rival. Indeed this species of history, stiled general, has at length become so acceptable, as to have given birth to another kind, not entirely diffimilar, which pretends not merely to relate facts, but to affign their caufes; which, as far as it fucceeds, muſt be highly agreeable to the reader, as well as honourable to the writer; fince to know facts themfelves is an eminent degree of knowledge; but to be acquainted likewife with their caufes, renders it at once both fatisfactory and complete.

The Scripture is in part, and in fome refpects, a general hiſtory. It relates events moſt important; the creation, deſtruction, and renovation of the world: it predicts the final fate that is to confume it, and announces the new heavens and the new earth which are afterwards to fucceed. Its firſt book contains the hiſtory of the antediluvian world, and the tranfactions of mankind ere they were diſtinguiſhed into tribes, or difperfed, as nations, over the face of the earth; and though it principally confifts of the hiſtory of a particular people, yet were *they*, by fome way or other, as allies, fubjects, or captives, connected with all the moſt confpicuous nations that have appeared from the beginning of time. Nay, if affigning the caufes of the moſt material events renders it fo, it is likewife a philofophical hiſtory; fince it is copious in dwelling on

caufes

causes not only such as are human, but also such as are divine. It represents the supreme Being as the remote, if not the immediate cause of all events; describes him as intent upon this end, the punishment of the wicked, and the remuneration of the righteous; and declares that he combines all events in this world, so that they may tend to the introduction of a better, and of an heavenly state, for which the present sufferings of his elect but the more effectually prepare and qualify them.

Well were it if all other histories were employed in investigating, and in descanting upon the same causes, and in exemplifying their apparent effects. What encouragement to virtue would thence ensue! What abashment of vice! But this would not be gratifying to the rich, the powerful, the luxurious. The general cry against such a writer would be, " In " thus saying thou reprovest us;" nay, the authors being, as they commonly are, vicious and depraved, by writing in the cause of virtue and religion, they would reprove themselves. It were indeed less blameable in them, and attended with less injury to mankind, were they to content themselves with passing over, unnoticed, what is against their present interest or inclination; but having felt the restraints

ſtraints of Revelation diſagreeable and burthenſome to themſelves, and known that they were ſo to others, they are led to imagine, that if neglecting it would in ſome degree promote their profit and popularity, reviling, contemning, and miſrepreſenting it, would advance them more.

Hence they combine in attacking the writings which contain it, in the moſt impious and illiberal manner; and take advantage of the loweſt and moſt ſpecious arts to degrade them. Being clothed and conveyed in a ſtile and manner different from modern, and profeſſedly hiſtorical works, they accuſe it of not attending to rules which it never preſcribed to itſelf; and which, when many parts of it were conſigned to writing, were not yet invented. They attribute errors to the original, which can only be aſcribed to the tranſlation; being delivered down in a language not generally underſtood, they miſquote, miſapply, and garble paſſages as it beſt ſuits their purpoſe; and from inattention to the cuſtoms, or manners, of the times in which theſe books were written, they repreſent things as ridiculous, which only appear ſo becauſe different from preſent uſage and modern practice. As to the aſſignment of cauſes, far from
recurring

recurring to the first and supreme, their principal pains are employed in entirely excluding all consideration of him. Instead of investing him with an irresistible controul over second causes, they never seem so highly gratified, as when they can represent *them* as independent of, and entirely effectual without, him. They attribute that to human counsels, which could only be the result of divine Wisdom, and elevate partial into complete causes; as if the subordinate could produce their effect, without the command or permission of the prime and principal.

Yet is the Scripture the power of God to make us wise unto Salvation; his word will stand the test of examination, criticism, sound learning. The assignment of causes in other writings is at best suspicious, since though those of recent transactions may be discovered from collateral circumstances, or from still existing instruments of information; yet what ingenuity, or application, can possess themselves of all the documents necessary to investigate the causes of events in very distant periods? This knowledge therefore, like all others which contribute to human vanity, is built on very slight and uncertain foundations. Not so that which is derived from the Scripture;

ture; whatever *that* assigns as the cause of any event, may be depended upon as being actually so. Its reflexions come home to every man's bosom; unless we make it a rule of conduct, we shall not only be unwise, but miserable: it assorts with every dictate of right reason and prudence; and to act in contradiction to it is not merely folly, but madness.

And if the writings of the Old Testament *singly* were supposed able to make the reader wise unto salvation, so must those, in a more eminent degree, of the New also. It was certainly the former to which St. Paul ascribes such a power in his Epistle to Timothy; yet we must suppose that he had respect likewise to the additions and improvements made to it by the Gospel, although the Canon of Scripture was not completed, nor the writings of the new yet joined to the old, at the time when this Epistle was written. And indeed it equally concerns us to defend the truth of both Covenants; nor is one jot or tittle of the law to be given up as of dubious or suspicious authority; for if Revelation may be false in one instance, it may in all, and thus forfeit every claim to veracity. Whatever seeming difficulties therefore, or inconsistencies appear in either, must be resolved into the error of the copyists,

copyists, or ascribed to a still imperfect acquaintance with the learned languages: but these difficulties daily disappear, as we make greater proficiency in these studies. The obscurities indeed are not immediately dispelled, that we may be encouraged to proceed, by meeting success proportioned to our application; and by the breaking in upon us, as we advance, of brighter and still brighter rays of light.

Yet with how little show of reason the Scriptures are accused of being false or unfounded, will appear from reflecting, that, notwithstanding the constant attempts to invalidate their authority, they still continue to constitute the firm and immoveable basis of historic truth. Notwithstanding the vain endeavours of nations, most remote from the country where the events they record are said to have happened, or otherwise most enlightened, to conceal it, still traditions, seemingly most national and peculiar to them, may be traced to the sacred writings as to their genuine source; an application to *them* removes the veil from whatever is mysterious in their ceremonies, unintelligible in their mythology, and extravagant in their pretensions to antiquity. The main principles of revealed religion,

gion, the most genuine accounts of the origin and creation of the world and its first inhabitants, though derived from the Scripture, yet being to be found, somewhat disfigured indeed, almost throughout the universe, as well attest the truth of the doctrine that all mankind are descended from a single individual, as speak the extensive and nearly universal dissemination of these traditions; which, like the grand properties of magnetism and electricity in nature, pervade the whole mass of human intellect, especially when it is polished by attrition, as it were, and its energies are awakened by society and civilization.

The Jews were selected by the Almighty for the express purpose of preserving, for a time, among themselves, the records of divine Revelation, and that afterwards they might be the means of communicating them to mankind in general. Their being at length rendered subjects to the Romans, must have sufficiently acquainted that great and renowned people with their tenets and pretensions. The history of the Roman, together with that of the latter Greek or Constantinopolitan empire, ere it was subdued by the Turks, comprehends a period of above two thousand years; a portion of time equal to a third part of the age of the

the world. Records so copious, so antient, so extensive, constitute of themselves a kind of general, as well as a considerable share of particular history, since the Romans were, by some means or other, connected with most of the then discovered nations; nay, but for the conquests of the former, the latter had been scarcely known beyond the limits of their own country. But the Roman empire, in its rise and decline, as well witnessed as partook in most of the important and interesting events that appeared on the theatre of the universe; it saw the sun of science slowly attain its meridian, and afterwards rapidly set in the long night of barbarism and ignorance: as it advanced, it observed the birth of the Christian Religion, its establishment, its corruption; and those who fled from that empire when tottering to its fall, partly contributed, by their successful labours, in the revival and more extensive communication of learning, to its subsequent reformation. Here then, namely in the history of that nation, and particularly of its decline, was a wide field for infidel writers to disseminate their doubts, and insinuate their suspicions; supporting them from authors, many of whose works are by this time nearly antiquated, and in reading which few
would

would possess the patience and application necessary to pursue and confute them. Yet some, animated by a laudable zeal, have followed them, and with considerable effect; and whoever shall afterwards succeed them in the same career, will continue to deserve well of mankind, and of our common Christianity, and they may fairly promise themselves that their labours will be equally useful; for the errors already detected afford a fair presumption that those which yet remain are capable of as easy a solution.

Ecclesiastical history, likewise, is infinitely involved with the other species; but the writers partaking of the disadvantages of the times in which they lived, and being mostly secluded and sequestered from the busier scenes of life, are not to be compared either in matter or stile with those of civil history. Indeed if the latter contains the vices or crimes of mankind, the former is swelled with the records of their folly and madness: so diligent, however, is evil, that accusations against Christianity are eagerly sought after, and produced from thence, yet with what shew of reason may appear from reflecting that few are capable of estimating their force, and fewer, if they could, are likely to be at the trouble of

rendering

rendering themselves completely masters of the subject. Until we are so, we must be content to believe those who have made it the sole and immediate object of their studies, when they inform us, that the objections against Revelation, as drawn from Ecclesiastical history, are such as very unfairly attribute the vices of Christians to Christianity itself; that it is charged with enormities which it never authorized, but constantly condemned; and that that is required from its commencement, and from its progressional state, which can only be expected at the period of its completion; namely, that folly and wickedness should be no more, and that unerring wisdom and perfect virtue should immediately appear.

When treating on general, and particularly on Ecclesiastical history, what shall we say of thee, Hypatia? The paragon of Heathen virtue and excellence, the constant theme of all succeeding writers, when desirous of degrading and of depreciating Christianity; whom the mob of Alexandria, in their blind zeal, cruelly and inhumanly destroyed. Such as thou wast, we lament that thou wast not ours: if thou canst at present be supposed sensible of revenge, thou hast it in the indelible stain fixed by a few ferocious individuals

on

on our profession; if forgiveness can be yielded to such an atrocity, and oblivion be suffered to bury it for ever, surely it might be granted in consequence of the grief, regret, and remorse of every sympathizing Christian who reads the story. Our religion may perhaps boast of daughters equally virtuous, but of none so accomplished, and at the same time so unfortunate. Yet thy unhappy fate is a proof, that the character of a religion is not to be taken from a single instance or two, but from its general effect in improving the manners and in promoting the happiness of mankind. It evinces the necessity of something more than human to subdue corruptions so rooted, and dispositions so depraved; it discourages all prospects of perfection here, and teaches us to expect it only when God shall finally select his jewels, rejecting such as are false and fictitious, and reserving only those of pure and genuine lustre.

To rescue then the Scripture and our common religion from the cavils and misrepresentations of some popular writers, is my design in these Lectures; in which, as to succeed, is most honourable, so to fail would perhaps not be entirely disgraceful, since the intent would in some degree apologise for the execution. It were likewise desirable that the minds of the younger

younger part of the present audience especially were rendered duly sensible of the dangerous designs of such authors; and to this nothing could more contribute than a suitable exposure of their various errors, subterfuges, and inconsistencies. Be it farther observed, that those evils are thus stated in the only place capable of effectually remedying them; for our situation naturally exempts us from the temptations which tend to produce vain, frivolous, and irreligious writings. Enjoying from the liberality of others a limited, yet philosophical, competence, the improvement of reason being one principal end of our studies, trained and nurtured from our very youth to the hopes and expectations afforded by religion, we can have no inclination to seduce, deceive, or to corrupt others, and undermine, at the same time, their temporal and eternal interests. Nay, it is incumbent on us not only to discourage the designs of those who are busy in depriving men of the hopes of salvation, but also to exert ourselves to the utmost in opposing and counteracting them, as well by confirming those in their pious resolutions, who adhere to the Gospel, as in recalling those to it who have miserably departed from and deserted it: *this*, love to our species, respect for our religion, and gratitude to our benefactors, most loudly demands from us. And, indeed, this place has never been deficient in producing advocates in the cause of Truth. The most learned of our members have always been most religious. ᵃ One particularly is alluded to, that others may follow; an example in all respects so conspicuous, who died as a Christian should, in the act of devotion, on his knees, and with his face towards heaven; who, after having been tinctured with all science, and having acquired almost every language, antient, modern, particularly the oriental, was known to declare, that, after all his most extensive researches, he found the Bible the best book, most instructive, most important, most worthy of the attention of mankind in general, and of scholars in particular. To excite defenders of these writings, as well as opponents to their adversaries, seems to have been the intent of the pious Founder of this Lecture; and being such, there is none of sober consideration but must be satisfied with its support, and rejoice in its continuance.

ᵃ Sir William Jones.

SERMON II.

MARK xiv. 59.

But neither so did their witness agree together.

A LOVE of singularity, and a prospect of advantage, have generally produced immoral and licentious writers: but whence are mankind so prone to approve and admire their writings? Alas! it is because they coincide with their vicious propensities, and, for a time at least, justify them to themselves. Of this none took more advantage than a foreign writer [b], highly celebrated for his labours in the walk of general history, of which so much has been said in the preceding discourse; and though it may seem indecorous to call in question the reputation of the dead, yet authors may be esteemed alive while their works are

[b] Voltaire.

so; at least, if depraved, the mischief which they occasion survives them to a period beyond all possible calculation. The statement then of the errors and misrepresentations of such literary productions as tend to corrupt the morals, and consequently to undermine the happiness of mankind, though it may be considered as an oblique accusation of the authors, yet is it, in reality, the defence of all that is good, important, and valuable.

Nay after all, to a certain degree the merits of this extraordinary writer must be acknowledged. Few or none ever possessed abilities so various, talents so engaging, and a vivacity so inexhaustible. In modern history the pre-eminence to all others would be particularly appropriate to him, were his authorities to be depended upon, or his veracity equal to the fertility of his genius, or to the brilliancy of his imagination.

An acute reasoner[c] has reduced to a few propositions, at most four, all that is necessary to evince the truth of Christianity, and to remove the doubts of the sincere, but scrupulous. Something similar is intended with respect to this so popular an author; and if,

[c] Leslie.

SERMON II.

from a few specimens, it shall appear that he was remarkably deficient in that which constitutes the character of a faithful, judicious, and legitimate historian, we may fairly argue from what we know to what we do not, and bestow less attention, when we next read them, upon his calumnies against Christianity; nay very rationally suspect our judgment, when we shall be inclined implicitly to confide in him, and to honour him with unqualified and unlimited approbation.

Cruelty is a disposition incompatible with a just conception of the Deity; only the weak and wicked, not the good and powerful, are so: yet this author has presumed to insinuate such an accusation against the Father of Mercies himself: and this he builds as well on the general[d] spirit of the Jewish polity, as on some particular national measures in obedience to it. The earlier ages of the world, ere science was matured, and refinement and civilization were known, necessarily sanctioned their laws with greater severity than those who are softened by long established social intercourse, humanized by the exercise of mild and courteous manners, and who have been trained

[d] Vid. Lettres de quelques Juifs, p. 22.

under the guardian care of a judicious and approved education. The character of invaders too, in which the Jews were at first conspicuous, rendered them more ferocious, than those who have for a considerable time enjoyed peaceable and uncontested possessions. But as to the acts of seeming cruelty recorded as taking place in consequence of the immediate command of God, they must be resolved into the necessary measures of the Theocracy, as well for the preservation of internal order, as to prevent external dangers. Thus in every wise government cruelty, as it may appear towards a few guilty individuals, is mercy to the public at large. Thus the retaliation was just, when those who had contaminated the bosom of the earth with innocent blood, were themselves to be extirpated: and thus as Agag's sword had rendered women childless, the divine Justice caused that, by the signal vengeance inflicted on him by the hand of Samuel, his mother also should be childless among women.

‘ Except in these, and perhaps a few other instances, we may venture to pronounce, that even the Revelation to the Jews is replete

e Ibidem, p. 32.

with

with mercy, benevolence, and compassion. They were not enjoined such barbarous rites as human sacrifices, according to our author's confident assertion, any more than criminals executed in the present day can be said to be sacrificed: such offerings indeed are the very crimes for the punishment of which they were commissioned by the Almighty to supersede the idolatrous nations of Canaan. Neither is it true that every thing devoted to the service of God was sacrificed. The cattle certainly might bleed upon the altar [f]: not so the men and women; they were only reserved for the menial offices of the Temple. Indeed the Jewish code enjoins the greatest moderation in the use of victory; it strengthens and secures what has since been considered as the law of nature and of nations. The manifesto of Jephtha, for instance, ere he attacked the Midianites, is a model for all who should hereafter find themselves in a similar situation. The reception, particularly, that is commanded to be given to strangers; the attention shewn by the Jewish law to the very cattle, and even to the trees of a conquered country, are but

---

[f] Ibidem, p. 316.

so many traits of mercy, exhibited in their policy; and which speak the divine Author patient, benevolent, plenteous in mercy and compassion.

But those who enjoy the confessedly milder revelation through Christ, cannot complain, because it follows another necessarily more severe; since as to them the latter is set aside, and become nearly obsolete; neither would they have considered the objections against it, as far as the accusation of cruelty is concerned, as in any degree affecting them, had they duly attended to the subject, nor been misled by the desultory and superficial remarks of profane and irreligious authors.

[g] With his usual alertness the writer at present under consideration asks, " is nature " changed since its origin; or to what else shall " we attribute the pretended power of magi- " cians to charm even serpents, as we are told " they could, in the Jewish writings?" No; nature is not changed, nor are there now wanting those that can " *handle any deadly* " *thing, and it shall not hurt them*;" and that not by divine interference, but through causes

[g] Ibidem, p. 339.

merely

merely natural. It is well known that there is an herb[h] growing in moſt quarters of the globe, that, if applied, can endue men with this power. There is therefore no occaſion for any change of nature for that purpoſe; and the queſtion of our author is as impertinent as it is ill-founded.

[i] The cities of Sodom and Gomorrah, ſays he, " were metamorphoſed into a lake of " brimſtone; as was the wife of Lot into a " pillar of ſalt, and Nebuchadnezar into a " bull." But were ſuch metamorphoſes confined only to the times of the Scripture? Do not Africa, Aſia, Sicily, Italy, by dreadful tokens, and more recent examples, ſhew that hurricanes, volcanos, earthquakes, lightning, can convert animals into ſtones, and cities into lakes of fire? As to Nebuchadnezar, it is true, we read that he was deprived of his reaſon; but that he was converted into a bull, we are at a loſs to diſcover. This may be ridicule; but where it is unſuitably introduced, it recoils upon the profane author; as in this caſe it indiſputably does.

[h] Ariſtolochia Anquiceda.
[i] Lettres de quelques Juifs, p. 342, 343.

" Wilt

[k] "*Wilt thou not possess that which Chemosh thy God giveth thee?*" said Jephtha to the King of the Amorites. Here, observes our author, is an instance of a Jewish leader acknowledging another God, besides the true. How so? Is it uncommon to argue with a man on his own principles, and for a moment to suppose that true which one knows to be false? This is all that Jephtha does on this occasion; and no great advantage to the cause of infidelity can be derived from it.

Our author in another place proceeds thus: When Naaman the idolater [l] demanded of Elijah, whether it were allowed him to enter the Temple with his master, and to worship the idol there with him, the Prophet only answered, Go in peace.

On which statement we can only observe, that he could be no longer an idolater, when he entered after this transaction into the Temple; since he is now supposed formally to renounce such a false kind of religion. As to worshipping the idol, that is superadded, no expression of that sort being to be found in the Scripture; and as to the Prophet's permission, that can by no force be extended be-

---

[k] Ibidem, p. 250.   [l] Ibid. p. 335.

yond

yond the performance of his duty, as an attendant on the royal perfon.

^m The books of the Jewifh Scripture, being the oldeft extant, have fuffered much from mutilation; and being written in a language only confined to the learned, are liable to be mifinterpreted. Hear our author's obfervation on this fubject! " You ought to know " that all the books of the Jewifh Scripture " were neceffary to the world; for how could " the fupreme Being infpire ufelefs books? If " then they were neceffary, how came they " to be loft or mutilated?" But is one obliged to allow that all the books of the Jewifh Scripture were neceffary to the world? This nobody has ever advanced, or even imagined, except himfelf.

Befides, muft books be always neceffary, and to the whole world, to render it probable that God fhould infpire their authors? May not fome be ufeful at certain times, and to particular perfons, and yet be not unworthy of being dictated by God? Befides, can any one prove that the writings now loft were not ufeful at the time, and to the perfons for whom they were compofed?

^m Ibid. p. 379.

There is likewise a distinction to be made between being useful and being necessary; being useful to the world, and to some certain persons. To confound these terms is not to reason accurately; and it had been as well perhaps, had our author pointed out such books as are counterfeit. Surely none esteemed canonical are so, unless he assigns to the term counterfeit a meaning very different from the common.

[n] This judgment too of the Jewish writings is hazarded by one in no degree conversant with the originals; else would he not have made the comment he has upon the prophecy of Malachi, *for* [o] *from the rising of the sun even to the going down of the same my name is great among the* Gentiles, *and incense is offered to it*; *for my name is great among the Gentiles*. So it runs in most translations, and our author objects to it accordingly, as being inconsistent with truth: yet the difficulty is removed in the English Bible, by substituting the words *shall be*, for the term *is*; and this is warranted by the genius of the Hebrew language, which often expresses the future by the present.

---

[n] Ibid. p. 332.   [o] Mal. i. 11.

[p] He revives likewise the stale objection, that the Almighty threatens, in the Jewish Scriptures, *to visit the sins of the fathers upon the children*; but this has been often defended and vindicated, since it is not the *ordinary* method of God's proceeding: he only acts thus when the son persists in the father's wickedness; for, according to the general rule of God's justice, the wickedness of the wicked rests in its consequences upon him, as the righteousness of the righteous does upon him.

"*I gave them statutes that were not good*" —how incompatible this, remarks our author, with the divine clemency, wisdom, or justice! But these bad statutes, as they are called, are merely given them because they did not obey the good; by way of reproach only; as after having forsaken the true God, they are directed to have recourse for aid to false deities. Nor are they literally statutes, but figuratively so: they were really war, famine, pestilence, captivity; the severe and awakening lessons which God may very rationally be supposed to introduce after milder and more lenient have failed.

[p] Vide Lettres de quelques Juifs, p. 344.
[q] Ibid. p. 346. Ezek. xx. 25.

Proceed

Proceed we now to more extravagant errors, scarcely compatible with common sense, much less with superior and brilliant abilities; were it not usual with divine Providence to make foolish the wisdom of the wise when opposed to him; to render even diviners mad, and to entrap the wicked in their own wickedness.

^r " The cherubims," says he, " are put into " the ark;" than which what could be a more egregious or ignorant mistake? How would a similar one, in another writer, have excited his sovereign contempt, and his ingenious ridicule! The ark was a chest two cubits high, and a cubit and an half broad; but the cherubims of Solomon were ten cubits high, and measuring from wing to wing ten cubits also wide: they therefore *stood* upon the ark; but it was impossible, such being their respective dimensions, to put them into it.

^s He likewise taxes the author of the book of Wisdom with a desertion of truth, when he thus wrote with respect to Joseph, and the divine Wisdom that conducted him: " *When* " *the righteous was sold, she forsook him not;* " *but delivered him from sin; she went down* " *with him into the pit, and left him not in*

^r Ibid. p. 361.   ^s Ibidem, p. 367.

" *bonds*

"*bonds till she brought him the sceptre of the kingdom*[t]." Here, says our author, according to this description he must have supplanted Pharaoh; which was not actually the case. Now the original must mean by the sceptre, no more one appropriated to a king, than an ensign of delegated authority: such were common in the East, as they are among us. By such a way of reasoning, the same writer might infer that a provincial magistrate, because preceded by a mace, was an emperor, or that a judge or chancellor, because attended with the same emblem of power, was a king.

Your patience is requested, while some of our author's manifest and palpable contradictions are introduced[u]. He endeavours to disprove the Pentateuch; that is, denies its being written by the acknowledged author, because the art of writing in his time was not yet known by the Jews, or by any other people; yet in a different place, speaking of Sanchoniathon, he says, " that his age was contempo-
" rary with the latter years of Moses; but the
" former confesses one part of his history to be
" taken from Thot, who flourished eight hun-
" dred years before the time of Moses." Thus

[t] Wisdom x. 13, 14.   [u] Ibid. p. 99.

he

he proceeds. "This declaration is one of the moſt curious that antiquity has left us, ſince it proves the uſe of alphabets eight hundred years before the time of Moſes." What, then, were they known ſo long before him, yet unknown at the time he wrote the Pentateuch? Was ever contradiction more glaring and obvious?

The writers, whom the ſame author quotes in ſupport of his objections, affirm, according to him, "that at the time of Moſes they wrote on ſtone, on lead, and on wood." He himſelf further declares, "that the Chaldæans engraved their obſervations upon brick," apparently while it was yet ſoft; "and the Egyptians *their* writings upon marble and upon wood." According then to theſe his writers, and according to himſelf in another place, ſtone was not the only material on which they wrote. But the cauſing of books to be engraved on ſtone, becauſe they could not otherwiſe be made, is a contradiction in itſelf; for if Joſhua, for inſtance, had dictated to the engravers every word, he muſt have been endued with patience ſcarcely credible. In that caſe, to have diminiſhed the trouble, it had been preferable to engrave them himſelf. That he did this, is not ſo much as pretended; but if the engravers

gravers worked after a copy, that copy muſt have been impreſſed upon ſome other material, contrary to the hypotheſis that there was no other.

Indeed it is needleſs for him to appeal to other writers to atteſt the truth of his aſſertions, ſince, whenever he wants authorities, he makes them. Yet one there is, namely, Luitbrand, the licentious Biſhop of Cremona, whoſe abominable calumnies he propagates, and whoſe ill-founded aſſertions he ſtill repeats (if indeed the works that bear the name of that Prelate are actually his), particularly his account of the ^w infamous Marozia, and of the Prelates of the Church ſaid to be deſcended from her. The See of Rome is indeed expoſed to reproach enough, and juſtly too, for her real errors, and ſhameful deviations from the purity of the Goſpel, without loading her with unmerited cenſure. Yet our author has not the ingenuouſneſs to acknowledge the *inſufficiency* of his materials, and that the writer from whom he derived his information was held in ſuch low eſteem, as well by his contemporaries as by thoſe who ſubſequently treated of the ſame ſubject, that they rather

---

^w Hiſt. Gen.

D

choſe

chose to neglect, than attend to communications in all respects so little worthy of belief or confidence.

His calculations, a specimen or two of which it is intended to exhibit, are as inaccurate as his other arguments are inconsistent and inconclusive.

Our author[x] supposes the prey taken from the Midianites, whether men or cattle, as mentioned in Scripture, to be more than the country could produce or support. But allowing his measure just, namely about an hundred square miles, yet the capability of a country to produce corn or cattle, depends more on the skill and industry of the inhabitants than on its extent: besides, both calculation and experience attest that it is possible for the same quantity of land both to exhibit such a population, and to maintain such a stock of cattle, as is attributed to it in Scripture. But that he was probably mistaken as to the dimensions, may be inferred from his actually confounding it with another country, of indisputably larger extent: for thus in a different work he proceeds. How ungrateful was it in Moses, after having received signal services

---

[x] Vide Lettres de quelques Juifs, p. 263.

from the High-prieſt of Midian, after having been admitted to the honour of marrying his daughter, and having been guided through the defart by his ſon, in return for ſo much kindneſs to devote the Midianites to deſtruction! But the truth is, the Midianites, among whom Jethro was High-prieſt, and thoſe whom Moſes conſigned to plunder, were different people. One lived near the lake Aſphaltites, the other on the Red Sea. Thoſe belonging to Jethro deſcended from Midian, the ſon of Chus; the other from Abraham, by Keturah. The former retained ſome knowledge of the true God; ſince we read of Jethro's offering ſacrifices to him. This reproach of his, therefore, againſt Moſes, is without foundation; and from this manifeſt miſtake with reſpect to the two countries, we may judge of his calculations in other inſtances, and may be convinced that, notwithſtanding his cavils, the aſſertion of the Scripture, with reſpect to the population and number of cattle, is accurate and juſt.

[y] The wealth left by David to Solomon, the immenſe profit returned from the merchandize ſent to Ophir, all in their turn fall under our

[y] Ibid. p. 292.

author's

author's critical sarcasm. According to modern, or rather European ideas, such profits may indeed appear extraordinary; but not under an absolute or Asiatic government. It is well known, that commerce at its infancy, or where a new source of it is opened, is attended with returns most astonishing; and this was probably the case in antient, as it certainly is in modern times.

Ere we part from this celebrated writer, it will be necessary to revive one accusation to which he is particularly obnoxious, which is most subversive of his own reputation, most prejudicial to his readers, and in its consequences most alarming to the cause of morality and religion; namely, his frequent, and indeed disgusting violation of decency and decorum. Providence seems to have fixed on this author, and his too numerous imitators, such an obvious and apparent stigma, that all of any dignity of character, or purity of sentiment, might thence discern how much their writings tend to debase human nature, and might avoid them accordingly. Those who read frivolous and licentious writings for amusement only, and to beguile the time which they find oppressive, are less to be lamented, if through them they become the victims of corruption; though it might be wished,

wished, that, even in this instance, innocence might be preserved. But when those whose aim is intellectual improvement, and who seek it in the delightful walks of general history, find those reptile sentiments of impiety and indecency cross their way, even should they escape their venom, the circumstance must strike them with horror and dismay. For to this our author, it is principally to be ascribed, that succeeding writers, seemingly remote from the temptation, are not satisfied with being immoral and profane, unless they are likewise indecent and licentious; so that purity of manners, the first and best effect of education, is never sufficiently secured, since the very books recommended to the rising generation, for promoting and preserving it, only tend to debauch and corrupt them more.

To follow this celebrated author through all his publications, would require works of equal magnitude and multiplicity with his own; not that a portion of an hour, but that a whole life were devoted to that purpose. However it is hoped that enough has been said to evince that he is what himself has pronounced concerning a rival writer, " one who " quotes falsely, whose authorities are not to " be depended upon, and who is ready, with
" equal

" equal sincerity, to take either side of the
" question;" and that not the witnesses against
our Saviour were, in their attestations, more
inconsistent with each other, than is that
eminent writer, in his attacks upon the Scriptures, at variance with himself.

Nor let it be objected, that not all that has
been produced on this occasion is for the first
time urged and insisted upon. The aim here
is not ostentation, but use. New arguments,
like green wood, may yield and start; but the
old, like seasoned rafters, as well strengthen as
support the building. Yet perhaps it has not
been before observed how very differently the
latter part of the life of an hero of his own
time and country, is described by our author
and by his biographer. By the former, the
decline of that extraordinary man is represented
as marked with no remains of the once illustrious Condé^e, but what must have occasioned
regret at the ruin of so great a man. By the
latter he is described as spending the evening
of his life in the bosom of friendship, amidst
the comforts and consolations of domestic and
literary conversation, and as closing his career
of earthly fame with hopes of more perma-

^e Histoire Générale.

nent

SERMON II.

nent glory in the heavens *which fadeth not away*. The exemplary death of such extraordinary men instructs, convinces, confirms posterity in exhibiting constancy in the faith, particularly in the last and most trying hour; and had our author concluded his existence with an exit so resigned, so dignified, with expectations so full of immortality, even his impious doctrines had been somewhat countenanced by it. But the reverse was actually the case; for if the accounts are true, of all the horrid departures from life, none were ever equal to that of Voltaire; in fearful apprehension of judgment, and in extreme despair. But at that time he only could reflect on the speculative, not practical consequences of his published opinions. Could he have imagined but half the evils that have since resulted from their being adopted as a rule of conduct, to the subversion of all law, order, and religion, it must have sharpened the thorns with which his death-bed was planted, and added tenfold to the agonies of his alarmed and distracted conscience. The pernicious consequences of these writings, then, are sufficient to warrant us in making them the particular subject of our animadversion, and to vindicate the Ministers of the Gospel as well in exposing the weakness

weakness and wickedness of the principles which are built upon them, as in pointing out the malignity and malevolence of those who are busy in encouraging and disseminating them; lest they *who have turned the whole world upside down*, should haply be induced, in the plenitude of fury and devastation, *to come here also.*

SERMON III.

2 COR. iii. 4.

For while one saith, I am of Paul, and another, I am of Apollos, are ye not carnal?

ST. Paul asks the question; and if it might be addressed to those who were in some sort spiritual; to those who followed really evangelical teachers, yet who rather chose to be called after *them*, than after Christ, much more is it applicable to those who betray stronger symptoms of being carnal, and who are seduced and deceived by false ones. For the vain, the intemperate, the ambitious, have always been as eager to enslave the mind as the body; since influence on the former generally leads to complete empire over the latter, and the possession of all that belongs to it. But to promote such wicked purposes, it is often expedient to oppose long established opinions, and to subvert antient usages by the

introduction

introduction of strange and novel doctrines. Thus various alterations are proposed in bodies politic, and new modes even of religion are suggested, seemingly for the general good, but really to answer particular interested views. In pursuance of the same plan it is, that faith itself is combated by opinion, and reason and revelation are set at variance. But if any doctrine more than others affords a field for such attempts, it is that of the Trinity. Being confessedly abstruse and mysterious, the generality think themselves unconcerned in its defence: it is therefore most exposed to the attacks of adversaries; in weakening and misrepresenting it less opposition is expected; and impious and malevolent designs incur less danger of detection. Yet notwithstanding all attempts, still it maintains its ground; and the seemingly capital objections have been so ably answered, that, if what has been said by its learned defenders shall be generally retained in memory, there is no fear of any surmises being encouraged as to the certainty of its truth, or that we should suffer our faith to be shaken with respect to it.

[a] St. John wrote his Gospel a considerable

---

[a] Bishop Horsley's Tracts, p. 17.

time after the other Evangelists had completed theirs; that he might remedy their defects, and supply their omissions. He says, that Jesus Christ is come *in* the flesh. A modern Socinian [b], of no ordinary fame, supposes it should be *of* the flesh; but this is an alteration entirely his own, nor supported by the authority of any manuscript whatever. And who sees not the absurdity of St. John's insisting so strongly on Jesus Christ's coming *in* the flesh, had it not been in his power, as a divine person, to come in another way, and had not his coming in this manner been entirely voluntary? Such an expression, therefore, was with great propriety applied to him, inasmuch as he divested himself of the glory which he had with the Father ages before the world began; but his amazing condescension gave grace to the act, and infinitely enhanced the value of it.

[c] " There are three that bear record in " heaven," though a questionable text, yet is not so absolutely necessary to establish the doctrine of the Trinity, but that it is sufficiently supported from other parts of Scripture

[b] Priestley.   [c] 1 John v. 7.

without

without it. Although it be not found in *all* the exifting manufcripts, yet its authority cannot be entirely done away, till we are fure that the majority of manufcripts, as well loft as preferved, were without the obnoxious paffage. In the mean time, the triumph attendant on expunging this verfe from the facred writings muft be very incomplete, amidft fuch a cloud of other witneffes that concur in fupporting this important and myfterious doctrine.

It is further objected to this fundamental article of our faith [d], that it is but a revival of Platonifm. But if a fimilarity in this refpect exift between the Gofpel and that philofophy, it muft refult from the remains of antient tradition, as originally derived from Revelation, concerning the triple union in the divine nature. Though the doctrines are fimilar, yet they are by no means the fame; the Æons derived from the fupreme Being, according to Plato, being inferior to him, whilft the fcriptural fcheme, on the contrary, reprefents the Son equal to the Father as *touching his Godhead*. Whoever therefore defcribes Platonifm, particularly as far as this doctrine is concerned,

---

[d] Ibidem, p. 213.

as

as corresponding with Christianity, betrays an ignorance of both; and as well exposes his inability in letters, as his instability in faith.

The interpretation of the word *Logos*, in St. John's Gospel, as contended for by this opponent[e] to the Trinity, is built upon his misconception of Platonism. To detect therefore this error, it would be necessary to dwell longer in explaining that metaphysical system. But he has rendered this unnecessary, by introducing, very unfortunately for himself, Theophilus, Bishop of Antioch, thus speaking: "It is clear that when God said, Let us make man, he spake to nothing but to his own Logos, or Wisdom;" that is, according to our opponent, to nothing but himself. The original passage in the Greek is, that he spake *to* his Logos, and to his Wisdom; the substitution therefore of the disjunctive *or*, for the conjunction *and*, is, though entirely in his manner, yet unauthorised, and the passage, far from being an argument against, directly proves what it was intended to disprove; since the Father, speaking to his Logos and to his Wisdom, can mean nothing else than to his Son and to his **Holy Ghost**.

[e] Ibid. p. 228.

These

These are some of the direct objections; others more oblique are such as the following: "What is easiest to be understood, is most useful; therefore likeliest to be revealed by God, and to be most attractive of human regard." But if God be, as he certainly is, of an infinitely superior nature to man, is it not probable, that questions relating to him should be more mysterious than those in which only ourselves are concerned? Nay, there are properties belonging to humanity, and even to seemingly most inconsiderable objects, beyond the power of the most exalted understanding among men entirely to explain. If such difficulties accompany the consideration of *earthly things*, how much more are they to be expected in *heavenly!* True there are some acknowledged obscurities attending the doctrine of the Trinity; but surely not all things are so. Its moral purposes are sufficiently obvious, and the pre-eminent value of the sufferings of the divine nature, to atone for human offences, is too manifest to be insisted on.

It is further observed, that such mysteries are incompatible with the very idea of a revelation; nay render it an absurdity in terms—"For how can that be said to be discovered, "which

SERMON III.

"which still remains concealed?" But the Gospel is a revelation not solely in respect of the Trinity, but in relation to those other important doctrines, which before its appearance had so long continued to be concealed from mankind; among the rest, a resurrection to a future state either of happiness or misery, correspondently to the merit or demerit of our actions in this life. Such doctrines, and the duties resulting from them, are so clearly revealed in Scripture, that he who *runs may read them.* It is therefore according to the majority of its discoveries that the Scripture is said to contain a revelation; though there may be one or two tenets, perhaps, to which that name may not be so strictly and properly applicable.

Athanasius, according to the author at present under consideration, does not deny that the first Christians were Unitarians. Agreed; but does this prove they were so? By no means. Besides, the faith of the primitive Church enters not at all into his present question. He is speaking of the unbelieving Jews; and the reason assigned for their rejecting the Messiah, is their being so gross as to look for no more in him whom they expected, than a mere man; but as to the Jewish converts,

verts, they were not at all in the view of the alledged author. The omission, therefore, to assert that they believed in the Trinity, far from proving the first Christians Unitarians, affords a surmise in favour of the contrary opinion: for if the Jews were to be condemned, before they were converted, for expecting in Christ but a mere man, they must have been equally so, had they entertained such a degrading opinion of him after they were so.

Another argument is taken from Epiphanius's omitting to affirm that the Nazarenes, who, according to our author, " constituted " in a great measure the primitive Church," believed the doctrine of the Trinity. Now after observing that the Nazarenes, of whom Epiphanius speaks, were not the first converts to Christianity, but a sect half Jew, half Christian, that appeared immediately after the destruction of Jerusalem, and whose opinion could be of no weight as to the primitive doctrine, let us examine what Epiphanius remarks concerning them. " I cannot say whether they " think him a mere man, or whether they " affirm, according to the truth, that he was " begotten of Mary by the Holy Ghost:" if he could, he would have done so; as he did not,

there

SERMON III.

there is a presumption that they were rather of the latter and orthodox opinion, than the contrary; at least we may as rationally infer the one as the other: the silence therefore of Epiphanius, and the supposed opinion of the Nazarenes, are either irrelevant, or prove just the contrary of that which they are adduced to establish.

These Nazarenes, adds our author, were Ebionites: possibly the latter Nazarenes were so, but not those that in part composed the primitive Church; and that the latter were so called is an absurd assertion, since the Ebionites were not then known as an heretical sect, whose distinguishing doctrine was the unity of the divine nature, in contradiction to the Trinity.

The Apostles, it seems, taught this doctrine with great caution and circumspection; but this is likewise an argument against all the most approved modes of teaching, which always proceed from the elementary to the more abstruse parts, *from milk to strong meat:* but the apprehension of being detected in a falsehood, or convinced of art or cunning, was as far from the Apostles, as it is apparent in the adversaries of their doctrines. No; they seem throughout to have been plain and sincere men; yet they had been unfit for their commiffion, had they been unacquainted with the propereft method of executing it.

But what fay the opponents, particularly the grand and principal one? " What can be " a clearer proof of the fenfe of the Scrip- " tures, than the practice of the Church? " No fuch thing as the Trinity was believed " in the firft or early ages of it; the fenfe " therefore of the Scriptures muft be per- " verted, which in after-times have been pro- " duced in its favour."

In another place he argues otherwife. " The " Scriptures, when properly explained, do not " fupport the doctrine; it could not therefore " be the faith of the primitive Church." Firft, then, becaufe it was not the doctrine of the Church, he infers that it could not be fupported by Scripture; fecondly, becaufe it is not, as he fays, fupported by Scripture, he afferts that it could not be the doctrine of the Church. Both proofs afford the cleareft inftance of that falfe way of reafoning, which is called arguing in a circle. In the fame way the Papifts prove the authenticity of their Scriptures, from the fupremacy of the Church, as they likewife fupport the fupremacy of their Church by the authority of the Scriptures.

An

An author of this perſuaſion triumphantly aſks, " What political view could be more " anſwered by tranſubſtantiation, than by the " Trinity'?" The queſtion might at firſt perplex us, did not general hiſtory ſtep in to our aid; for the papal pretenſions to *Inveſti-ture* ſufficiently ſhew the ſtate effects intended to be produced by that abſurd tenet. It was no preſumption in him, who was habitually employed in making a God, occaſionally to make a King or Emperor; and the erecting of the ceremony of marriage into a ſacrament, at the ſame time that the Prieſts were reſtrained from it, who, if it were really ſo, are at leaſt as much entitled to it as the Laity, can only be accounted for on ſimilar grounds, not only as it contributed to the Church a conſiderable quantity of gifts and oblations, but alſo greatly tended to increaſe its power and influence: the ceremony might be permitted or prohibited, as beſt ſuited its intereſt, or the wiſhes of the wealthy, the powerful, and the luxurious. The degrees of conſanguinity are often difficult either to be eſtabliſhed or even to be diſproved. Here then was a conſtant field for appeals, always attended with expence in proportion to the wealth and importance of the parties; and here also a conduct was shewn, which might as fairly be taxed with worldly-mindedness as that of the Corinthians in the text; and, after having been fairly convicted of it, the Papists might with equal reason be asked, *Are ye not carnal?*

To return to the main subject, the observation is just, *that in science we are guided by reason, in history by facts*, which, if well ascertained, cannot be invalidated by subsequent argument; since, if the facts are once established, all reasonings against them are nugatory and superfluous. That a writer did not reprove a professed Arian, is no argument that he approved of his opinion; nor even should he occasionally, on a particular subject, commend him, is it a proof that he coincided with him in *all* respects: and if it is clear that Theodotus[g] was the first Arian, and that he lived at the close of the second century, it is vain to attempt to prove that the Trinity is a doctrine that sprung up subsequently to, and not at the origin of Christianity. The truth is, that the writers mentioned as commending Arianism, will be found on examination strongly to condemn

---

[g] Bishop Horsley's Tracts, p. 241.

demn it. The silence of authors on subjects not immediately connected with the Trinity, is abundantly atoned for by the fullest attestation in its favour, whenever it enters into the question. Besides, corruptions from the nature of the things are posterior to the institutions of which they are corruptions. Arianism being a corruption of the doctrine of the Trinity, could not be prior to it. *That* heresy then appeared two hundred years after the first preaching of the Gospel, and it proceeded no further than to declare the Son, though inferior to the Father, yet a divine person still, and a more important sacrifice than any human being could have been. It represented him at the same time the deserving object of praise and adoration. It was not till many centuries after that Socinianism carried this wickedness to the greatest length, debased, as far as it could, the most holy Messiah, deprived him of his divine nature, and infinitely diminished his power either to suffer for, or to save us.

It may be asked, whether moral duties are not preferably enjoined to speculative doctrines? Now, without admitting that of the Trinity to be merely theoretical, there may be a general or particular necessity for more than ordinarily dwelling upon it. When objections

jections against it are disseminated throughout the whole nation, it should operate as a call upon the Clergy, in a body, to be instant in season and out of season in inculcating the belief of it; and a similar necessity attaches upon the pastors of particular districts, in which the same negligence or contempt should unfortunately appear, otherwise our Saviour's injunctions, with respect to satisfying some duties, and omitting others, hold as to the insisting upon doctrinal, to the neglect of practical points: *this ought you to have done, and not to leave the other undone.*

The doctrine of the Trinity renders the holy Scriptures consistent, and removes the necessity of amendment or interpolation. Reference to the literal sense is alone requisite to reconcile all the parts of the Christian scheme. Grace, contrition, atonement, acceptance, are all well supported under the idea of a divine Mediator, and of a sacrifice more than human. But how is thinking matter consistent with an immortal soul? or how is a future judgment admissible on the supposition that the matter which, exclusively of the particle of the divine breath, forms one man, continually and successively composes others? In such a case, he has as little to do with the

matter

matter that formed himself, as with that which formed others; for deny the separate existence of the soul, and every principle of individuation is lost; and you might as well judge a multitude for the faults of one, as an individual for his own. Besides, what mere man can perform an unsinning obedience? can justify himself, much less others? Under such an incomplete idea, we should be at a loss for that perfection that supplies our deficiencies, and for that unsinning obedience which stamps a value on our otherwise imperfect services.

If then the doctrine of the Trinity has its difficulties, the Arian or Socinian scheme has more; as is manifest from the pains taken to support and give it currency, and from the astonishing perseverance of its advocates, who engage with wonderful audacity in the cause, and who, when according to every impartial judgment they should be perfectly convinced, then appear to be least so.

[h] " If the obnoxious doctrine of the Tri-
" nity," says its inveterate opponent, " were
" removed from the Gospel, it would more
" easily recommend itself to Infidels and Ma-

[h] Bishop Horsley's Tracts, p. 264.

" hometans."

"hometans." What then would he, who charges us with art and prevarication in the defence of it, advise us for any secondary purpose whatever to abandon it? We should then indeed be the proper objects of his scorn and reproach, and, which is more, incur the anger of our divine Master; besides, the commands of God are express against *handling the Scripture deceitfully*. If we must omit *this* doctrine to ingratiate ourselves with one set of men, and *that* to accommodate another, we might at length be brought by piece-meal to give up the whole Gospel. The resurrection from the dead, and an heaven affording such pure and refined joys as Christianity promises, would probably be as repugnant to the inclinations of a Mahometan, as the doctrine of the Trinity is to his preconceived notions of the divine Unity.

As to infidels, indeed, the preaching of Christ to them under the description of a mere man, and inculcating upon them the doctrine of the Unity, would be only teaching them what they knew, or might have known before; since Theism was the first and traditional religion of all mankind, ere idolatry and the Jewish revelation commenced; yet it answered no purposes of virtue or reformation.
When

When therefore the world, by retaining this apparent wisdom, knew not God, it pleased him to save it by the *foolishness of preaching*. True he might, as possessing infinite power and knowledge, have saved us in any other way; but it is right to suppose, that, as he is all perfect, the actual is the best possible way; at least he has not made us judges of his councils. In this, as in many other respects, all we have to do is to accept the gracious favour, without objecting to the terms, or canvassing the grounds of it: and as to infidels, it appears that if the knowledge of one God, while they retained it, could not preserve them true to their duty, the desertion of the doctrine of the Trinity, to introduce that of the Unity, is a measure that is neither expedient, nor likely to be successful.

And indeed great is this mystery of our religion, which human intellect is not able entirely to comprehend, nor accurately to explain; and if the three Persons in the Godhead are actually one, it must be in a manner of which we can form no idea; neither is it liable to the objection so frequently urged against it, " that *production* is necessarily prior " to the thing produced, and that cause and " effect can never be cotemporary;" since we

know

know that mind and thought exist together and at the same time, fire and light, and the object of sight and the perception of it [1]. But hold, lest, in our endeavours to explain this almost inexplicable mystery, we should be found presumptuous in the sight of the divine Majesty, by endeavouring to intrude into his more immediate presence, nay, to pry into his most august and inscrutable nature; nor let us incur the condemnation of attempting to be *wise above what is written*. And as to the doctrine of the Trinity, as far as it is an object of reason, let us admire and revere it; and as far as it is affirmed to be contained in the Scripture, let us assent to it in proportion to the support it derives from thence, which, though continually questioned and attacked, yet has never been effectually set aside.

Indeed arguments, or seeming arguments for that purpose, must be brought from remote antiquity, from historians profane or ecclesiastical, who wrote in languages now become either dead or nearly obsolete. The adversaries therefore of our faith have this advantage, that few will have the patience or diligence, and fewer still the abilities, to as-

---

[1] Bishop Horsley's Tracts.

certain the juftnefs of their remarks, and follow them through writings at beft unintereſting, generally unprofitable, and often difguſting. They are fure therefore of a temporary triumph, and that their adherents will not fail to give them credit for uncommon literature and fuperior erudition: yet, thanks be to God, our eſtabliſhment, in which all are not confined to the province of preaching, has always produced thofe, who have moſt honourably to themfelves, and moſt ufefully to the cauſe of Chriſtianity, devoted their labours to the vindication of fuch doctrines as might occafionally be queſtioned by the wickednefs and prefumption of the age; and *their debtors* the Chriſtian world is for many able defences of the feveral important tenets of the Gofpel. As to the Trinity, *that* in our days has been attempted to be fuperfeded, by one whofe perfeverance, abilities, nay, apparent virtues, might create apprehenfion to the moſt confident friends of religion: yet it has pleafed God to raife him up an antagoniſt, in moral qualifications at leaſt his equal, and in literature infinitely his fuperior, who has carried the advantages of victory even farther than could be expected, having refuted, detected, expofed, filenced him; and convicted him of
fuch

such arts, management, evasion, and subterfuges, as must disgrace any cause, and effectually damp the ardour of all those who shall in future presume to attack this most sacred doctrine. From this copious repository some arguments have been selected, which seemed most satisfactory, that those who have leisure and inclination may peruse the remainder, and that those who have not, nay, that the whole Christian world may concur in the general resolution, that if Paul, or Apollos, or even an Angel from heaven should teach any other doctrine than what has been preached, they will rather rely on the express declarations of the Scripture than on theirs, and that they may rest assured that their teachers have not taught them cunningly devised fables, but that the doctrine of the Trinity, in particular, is built upon grounds firm, solid, and hitherto unshaken. They are therefore, by every tie, moral, rational, and religious, obliged to hold fast the possession of their faith without wavering, to which they were solemnly pledged when they were baptized *in the name of the Father, and of the Son, and of the Holy Ghost*.

SERMON IV.

PROVERBS xxi. 30.

There is no Wisdom, nor Understanding, nor Council against the Lord.

THERE are many devices, saith another Scripture, *in a man's heart; nevertheless the council of the Lord, that shall stand.* One object of man's device, though not easily attained, is to reconcile to his conscience the unrestrained indulgence of passion: this he has constantly, but vainly attempted, almost from the birth of time. With this perverse propensity all writers, who prefer the gratification of their own vanity, or the acquisition of filthy lucre, to promoting the cause of truth and virtue, have generally endeavoured to comply. Nevertheless the dictates of conscience, and the according impressions of Revelation, have maintained their ground; and notwithstanding the wiles of wickedness, the asseveration

tion of audacity, and the infinuations of philofophy, falfely fo called, ftill the credibility of miracles, the proofs of Chriftianity for inftance, remains unfhaken and unmoved. They are as well attefted as any hiftorical fact; and it is very remarkable, that, though at prefent objections againft them are eafily produced and countenanced, yet at the time neareft to that in which they were performed, fufpicions as to their authenticity were never harboured or propagated. Shall we then prefer modern doubts to the conviction of the antients, who lived neareft the time of thofe extraordinary events, and who were confequently beft qualified to judge of them?

We have alfo a more fure word of prophecy, that is, which is attended with evidence more, if poffible, to be relied on by pofterity; which conftantly accompanies it, and acquires in every fucceeding age greater and greater ftrength. If thefe foundations, then, are firm and compact, they cannot yield to any other weaker and fubfequent fuggeftions.

The author of the Hiftory of the Decline and Fall of the Roman Empire has unhappily united a defire of gratifying the too general inclination to throw off all moral reftraint, to abilities in other refpects uncommon, and

to

to industry persevering and unconquerable. But in proportion as his aim seems to have been to depreciate our religion and its divine Author, so has it been to elevate, into unmerited consequence, a character most opposite and inimical to both; namely, the Emperor Julian, whose disposition he has so long studied, that he seems at length in some degree to have reduced his own to a similarity with it. For that apostate, when persecuting the Christians, was remarkable on such occasions for adding insult to injury [a]: he deprived them of their property, withal saying, "Be quiet, for "your religion forbids your pursuing legal "modes of redress." "Why," added he in the same spirit, "do you repine at sufferings? "Your God, has he not taught you to despise "the goods of this world, and to undergo with "patience afflictions and injustice?" And on another occasion he thus joins the most terrible menaces to a cold and malignant pleasantry. "What an admirable law is that of "the Galilean, which teaches his followers "to forego advantages on earth to arrive at "Heaven! We are determined, as much as is "in our power, to expedite their journey thi-

---

[k] Le Beau, Histoire du bas Empire, v. iii. p.180.

"ther."

"ther." In like manner this historian, avoiding the plain and direct road, endeavours to undermine all divine revelation, and is less easily to be guarded against, from his introducing suspicious surmise and rude raillery, rather than a consistent charge or open accusation.

Language perhaps has hardly a word more equivocal, than the common expression, *cause*; for it may either be partial, or total, material, formal, or final—either principal, co-ordinate, or subordinate ; nor till the precise sense of the word, among so many, is clearly ascertained, can we at all depend on the accuracy of the author's reasoning who uses it. Causes too, and those eminently effectual, are often too mean to correspond with the dignity of history to mention them ; others are so concealed, that, though it may flatter the vanity of the political historian to suppose that he has discovered them, yet, as they often elude the search of contemporaries, we cannot repose great confidence in the pretended knowledge of those, who, in after-ages, conceive that they have rendered themselves acquainted with them. In a posthumous publication, indeed, this confessedly agreeable writer has endeavoured to atone for the mischief done by his grand work ; and at last declares, that, in

his

SERMON IV.

his assignment of the causes that produced the success of Christianity, he meant only such as were merely human. Yet who sees not that his introduction of human causes was intended to render less necessary the interference of the divine and supreme; without which no human or subordinate one could possibly operate. If the former were to combine with the latter for unworthy purposes, it would derogate from its honour; and if by inferior causes it should promote effects to which they were of themselves inadequate, they would then be accidentally and improperly styled causes; but not so in the true and accurate sense of the expression.

The first cause alledged by this author for the extensive propagation of the Christian faith, which took place soon after its appearance[1], was a Jewish zeal against idolatry prevailing among the converts to the Gospel. But the Apostles first introduced it among their countrymen the Jews: how then could their patience and perseverance be excited by a zeal against idolatry, in converting a people among whom at the time it was not practised? In this case the cause is applied to an object

[1] Vide Bishop Watson's Apology for Christianity, p. 236.

which did not exist; it could not then be truly assigned.

Indeed the non-compliance of the first preachers of Christianity, with the customs and opinions of those, as well Jews as others, whom they attempted to convert, seems a method rather of estranging men from, than of reconciling them to, a new doctrine. So thought the Jesuits, and those sent out in modern time to propagate the Gospel in countries yet unconverted, who are generally taxed with accommodating too much the precepts of the Gospel to the customs of the people amongst whom they travelled; not as not practising the best means for effecting their purposes, but as deviating from the rectitude, and polluting the purity of the Christian faith. This they had not done, had they judged, with our author, that a fierce and intolerant zeal was the best method of propagating religious opinions, and of gaining converts to them.

[m] Under this head our historian infers, from the recorded disobedience of the Jews, under the very impression, as it is said, of the divine miracles, that they disbelieved both them and

---

[m] Ibidem, p. 248.

the revelation itself, in attestation of which they were performed. This observation, it is to be feared, is hazarded with the malicious intention of undermining the supports as well of the Jewish as of the Christian dispensation, or rather of piercing the one through the sides of the other. But the objection will lose its force with those who are sufficiently acquainted with the deplorable depravity of human nature. Alas! it is no argument that a man disbelieves a religion, because he *acts* in contradiction to it. Among the Jews, as among the Christians, there will always be found such as believe, yet tremble; who are obedient only while judgment impends over them, but who are continually abusing that Mercy, to which, at last, they must have recourse for pardon, if they would encourage any hopes of salvation; consistently with which expectation, though they may occasionally provoke the patience and long-suffering of God, yet they can never entirely reject and abandon it.

The partial or imaginary causes assigned by this celebrated historian, seem intended to depreciate, or rather to render unnecessary the real ones, recorded as the principal means of the succefs of the Gofpel; namely, the miracles of our Saviour, and thofe of his Apoftles.

[n] Now the fecond caufe, which, independently of them, he introduces, is the doctrine of a future ftate, and the expectation which was then encouraged of the prefent world being foon to be confumed. But though this apprehenfion was, in the fubfequent ages of the Church, applied to the enriching of convents, and other religious communities, yet in that light, and to that purpofe, it could not be ufed by the firft teachers of Chriftianity, fince it made no part of their doctrine. Of this there can be no greater nor more convincing proof, than the paffage of St. Paul in his Epiftle to the Theffalonians: "We be-
"feech you, brethren, by the coming of the
"Lord Jefus Chrift, and by our gathering to-
"gether unto him, that ye be not fhaken, nor
"troubled, neither by fpirit, nor by word, nor
"by letter, as from us, as that the day of judg-
"ment is at hand. Let no man deceive you
"by any means." How could that notion, then, namely, of the near approach of the day

[n] Ibid. p. 255.

of judgment, be a cause of the extensive acceptance of Christianity, which the Apostles themselves disowned and discountenanced?

° Nor could the doctrine of the Millennium, a similar reason assigned by our author, contribute to the same purpose; since among the primitive Christians it was only partially, and not universally entertained. It is a notion not less contrary to the opinion of many antient, than to that of the most respectable modern writers: it rested therefore on too disputable grounds, and was confined within too narrow a circle, to be so extensively effectual as our author supposes it.

Neither was it the doctrine of a future state, as it is at this day professed among Christians, that was sufficient of itself to produce the wonderful effects that, at its first stages, attended the Gospel; for it promised not a state of bliss hereafter, consistent with the indulgence of impure and irregular passion here: it required the sacrifice of the dearest earthly interests, to qualify men for that perfect state to which it was intended to introduce them. It was not a merely spiritual existence which it announced to those who were obedient to

° Ibidem, p. 271.

it, but one in which the soul was again to be reunited to the body. This was contradictory as well to the general opinion, as to the result of constant experience. It was likewise attended, and strongly charged with circumstances of uncommon terror; such as the dissolution and conflagration of all things; considerations adapted rather to appal, than to conciliate, particularly the wicked, and which surely nothing could have engaged them to believe, but a conviction of the authority of those who taught such a doctrine, as well as of the conclusiveness of the proofs by which they evinced it.

*These proofs consisting of miraculous powers which, according to our author, were *ascribed* to the Apostles, but not actually possessed by them, or by their more immediate successors, are mentioned by him as another cause of its success.

But they are mentioned only to be misrepresented; and such false and pretended miracles, as *he* recounts, were never exhibited by the Apostles, but were introduced in after-ages by the subsequent corruptions of the Church. However be it observed, that those attributed to

P Ibidem, p. 276.

our

our Saviour and his Apoſtles in the New Teſtament, are ſo connected with the hiſtory of the Old, that they both muſt ſtand or fall together. Not ſo the falſe miracles introduced into other hiſtories: they have no natural connection with each other, or with either of the Teſtaments; nor are *they* at all concerned in their truth. Yet the forgery of, or pretence to miracles, far from ſubverting the credit of the true, actually eſtabliſh it. Were there none genuine, it never had entered into the mind of man to counterfeit any. In the ſame manner we may infer the actual exiſtence of numerous virtues, from the many attempts of hypocrites to impoſe upon the world by the empty appearances of them.

[s] Indeed preſent experience cannot invalidate the teſtimony of tradition in favour of miracles: not a man's own, becauſe that is very limited; not that of his friend, becauſe that is equally ſo. But if recourſe is had to the tradition of hiſtory, thoſe of all nations unite in bearing teſtimony to them, which cannot be rejected without denying as well *their* authenticity as that of the ſacred book,

---

[s] Ibidem, p. 285.

which the best judges have always declared to be the most genuine of any in the world.

The power of attraction in the magnet, ere it was known, was contrary to experience; but was that a good reason for denying it? Later experience has proved it true. Particular experience, therefore, is no more an objection against the suspensions of nature, as is the case in miracles, than it would have been against the discovery of powers before unknown; as is the case in the attraction of the magnet.

' The next cause assigned by this popular historian, is the virtue of the first Christians. But what he confers with one hand, he resumes with the other; the constant artifice of this seemingly candid writer: for the Gospel, according to him, was first addressed to women, to the ignorant, ⁵ to the polluted with atrocious guilt; and it was only from their desire of separating themselves from the rest of mankind, that the first Christians, like other sects, pretended to extraordinary purity. Now the majority of the converts were not such as this author has represented them. The Apostles

' Ibidem, p. 290.   ⁵ Ibidem, p. 291.

might have enumerated among them some of [t] the principal men of the then principal cities: they had no fellowship with the works of darkness, but rather reproved them; yet wherever a sincere desire of reformation appeared, to that they advised, invited, encouraged men; and if their religion afforded comfort and medicine to a few wounded consciences, it was rather a recommendation than a disparagement of it. True, many sects, but not all, have pretended to extraordinary piety; yet the purpose of the Apostles was not separation, but to form the whole world into one society, or rather to select out of it a *peculiar people zealous of good works*. They withdrew from the Jews only as far as they were wicked; and throughout all ages separation from the profane has never been reckoned a disposition to schism or sectarism. As to the Gentiles, it is manifest that the Apostolical invitation to union was particularly addressed to them; and how the Apostles could be said to be desirous of separating from those with whom they were never effectually united, is a question which may be left with those to determine

[t] Ibidem, p. 295.

who pin their faith upon the sleeve of this author.

The last cause by our historian assigned for the success of Christianity, is the wonderful union which he says subsisted among the first Christians. But this indeed, though they aimed at it, they could never accomplish: they were early and constantly subject to be broken into sects, and to be divided by a variety of opinions; nay the very persecutions which they endured tended to disunite them from those whose zeal was not the most warm, and who therefore, in time of afflictions, fell away.

"Not that the diversity of opinions, which still exist, can be fairly laid to the charge either of the primitive Church, or of the Reformation afterwards, as if they necessarily gave birth to it. Alas! it seems inherent in our nature. Truth certainly cannot be but one; yet wherever there are men, they will disagree, particularly as to its more abstruse points: in this they are generally determined more by their interests than their intellect. All too are naturally ill-disposed to whatever awes or restrains them; yet some follow more au-

---

* Ibidem, p. 300.

stere, others more relaxed modes of faith; and even the former act thus consistently with the before-mentioned hatred of authority, since it is often found that the more openly rigid are covertly the more licentious. But God, and he alone has a right to do it, produces good and advantage to the cause of religion even from evil. The various sects are certainly a check upon each other, and *false teachers* on the professors of the original and true doctrine. Thus, perhaps, virtue and religion, on the whole, derive some benefit from the energy and emulation which, respectively to recommend themselves, the different sects exhibit. But no merit is due to the authors of these divisions on that account; nor are the advantages equal to those that would accrue from the whole Christian Church's maintaining, as the Gospel directs, an **entire** harmony, and a permanent and uninterrupted peace, among all its members.

It is true, that in every Christian congregation a discipline prevailed, which it were well for the common religion, if it at present in a greater degree subsisted. None but those of good character it received, or who shewed signs of sincere contrition and repentance; and
the

the latter, after baptism, underwent a severe discipline of fasting, watching, prayer, and seclusion, ere they could be completely admitted into the bosom of the Church. But these severities, by the way, seem, unless supported by the other divine aids which the Apostles possessed, to have been rather discouragements than allurements to fresh converts to enter into it.

"As to the various regulations of the infant Church for the government of its members, this power of enacting them it possessed in common with all other societies; and with respect to them they were left by their divine Master to be guided by the dictates of their own prudence; the Gospel, as it contains no directions as to them, so neither is it concerned in the use of them. We must confess that there have been vicious priests, and biassed ecclesiastical councils, that have enjoined impious and irrational decrees. The Church of Rome too is likewise guilty of abominable errors, as well in opinion as practice; but as religion approves of none of these things, but expressly forbids them, so neither is she at all

---

^w Ibid. p. 312.

chargeable with them: let man bear the blame, but let divine Revelation remain spotless and unimpeached.

Yet it seems an unenviable ingenuity to take a mischievous pleasure in accumulating all that can be said against the first Christians, and at the same time to suppress all that might be urged in their favour; to blow into a flame each spark of calumny against them, and at the same time to extinguish the flagrant accusations which then subsisted against their adversaries. [x] The historian dwells with apparent satisfaction on the discovery that a reputed Saint was publickly accused of so mean a crime as that of theft, but, for purposes best known to himself, he conceals the circumstance that the charge was entirely false and ill-grounded; a conduct this, that by every impartial reader must be condemned, as a manifestly injurious suppression of a material point in the case; and such a charge rather confers reputation than ignominy on the accused, and on the cause in which he was engaged.

Not that his intention or sincerity makes the martyr, as is pretended by [y] a writer of a

---

[x] Gibbon's Miscellanies, Vol. II. p. 574.
[y] Voltaire.

somewhat similar stamp, but the absolute truth of the cause can alone entitle the sufferer to that sacred appellation. Our historian too, with an equally favourable disposition towards Christianity as usual, declares, that it first recommended itself to Constantine by the doctrines of passive obedience and non-resistance, which it inculcates; yet these were not known till many centuries after, when the Scripture precepts of loyalty to legal sovereigns were strained, as they always are by the spirit of party, to an unnatural extreme; but as to Constantine, he had none to contend with, who opposed him under the pretence of supporting the cause of liberty, except only rival candidates for the empire. No, that sacred flame was extinguished with the last heroes of the republic; nor has it ever since, to any purpose, revived in Rome pagan or papistical; nor has the latter ever pretended to it, till recently some modern writers of that persuasion have indeed surprised us[y], by attempting to reconcile civil liberty with political slavery, freedom of disquisition with papal infallibility, and the rights of man with the summary proceedings of the inquisition. But of this

---

[y] Vide History of Henry II. and Church and State.

more

more hereafter. In the mean time, how could the charge against Christianity, exhibited by the historian of the Decline and **Fall**, that it made citizens disobedient to the government, and soldiers mutinous, be consistent with what he says in the accusation just now mentioned, that its doctrines of passive obedience and non-resistance recommended it to the rulers of the present world? Surely these two accusations cannot **subsist** together. As to martyrs, there were certainly enough of them, who suffered sufficiently to establish the truth of their religion; [a] but the needless pains taken in endeavouring, by a very precarious [b] calculation, to reduce their number, to palliate, if possible, the cruelty of those who consigned them, though innocent, to such severe torments, betray a mind very manifestly biassed against our **most holy faith, and must take very much from all that a writer under such influence might assert in disparagement of it.**

What a parade is there made of the virtues, the erudition, the heroism of Julian, though one abominable method of **divination**, as practised by him, is entirely omitted, which yet

---

[a] Vide Gibbon.
[b] Vide Abridgement of Gibbon, Vol. II. p. 231.

is recorded by an ᶜ author, of whom the historian of the Decline and Fall has made frequent and liberal use; and with respect to superstition, though the first Christians are occasionally by this writer abundantly loaded with this accusation also, yet how is this reconcileable with the charge made against them by the same author, even of atheism itself? *That* at least, and superstition, are totally incompatible.

ᵈ They are accused likewise of conspiracies against the state; yet the very same author taxes them with meanness of spirit, with an idle and philosophical abstraction from worldly affairs, with an Epicurean pursuit of merely selfish gratification. Men thus disposed quit not usually their retirement, to encounter cares of any sort, much less to mingle in conspiracies.

ᶜ Muratori Annali d'Italia, Vol. II. p. 427. Così nel celebre Tempio di Carres dedicato alla Luna, per quanto narra Teodoreto *, chiusosi Giuliano un giorno durante la suddetta spedizione, non si seppe cosa ivi facesse, se non che uscito, mise le guardie a quel Luogo, con ordine di non lasciarvi entrar persona, fino al suo ritorno. Venuta poi la nuova di sua morte, fu aperto il Tempio, e vi si trovò una donna impiccata col ventre aperto, per qualche incantesimo fatto da Giuliano, o pure per cercar nelle di lei viscere quel, che gli dovea succedere nella guerra co' Persiani.

ᵈ Bishop Watson's Apology, p. 343.

* Lib. 3. H. c. 21.

They

SERMON IV.

'They are likewise injuriously charged with the commission of the most atrocious crimes. How then, according to our author, could they recommend their religion by their apparent virtues? But the falsehood of this accusation is abundantly proved, by the yet extant Epistle of the younger Pliny to the Emperor Trajan, who, so far from confirming this calumny, declares concerning them, ' " that " they were a description of people who bound " themselves by an oath not to commit any " wickedness, who met periodically, and sang " hymns unto Christ as unto God, and after a " temperate repast retired." Here then is the so much required testimony of an Heathen to the character of the first Christians, and, what is more, it attests their innocence.

So weak and inconclusive are the reasonings of otherwise learned men against the Lord, and against his anointed! The few selected may serve as specimens of the rest; and doubtless their other councils, were there time or inclination to examine them, would prove equally frivolous and unfounded. Councils did I say? It is an abuse of the term: they

---

ᵉ Ibidem. Ibidem, p. 247.

are

are but the despicable effusions of depravity and its usual attendants, artifice and misrepresentation. Nor does the whole discourse afford a more important inference, than the different effects of learning pursued for the purpose of justifying ourselves and others in the practice of wickedness, or for ever establishing men in the paths of virtue and righteousness. In the one case, the more we improve in solely human accomplishments, the vainer, and consequently the blinder we are rendered as to all the most useful and most important purposes of our being: in the latter, the more we know, the more virtuous we are; and the more virtuous, the more complete we become in all enviable and really profitable science, till at length upon the minds of such truth beams in meridian splendour, and the clouds of error and sophistry no sooner collect than they are dispersed: they are reproved of all, they are convinced of all, and falling down and worshipping, they are enabled to declare of the universe, as the devout Christian concerning the congregation of the faithful, *Surely God is in this place*; neither is their heart troubled, but believing in the supreme Being, they are consequently justified in believing

lieving alſo in him, whom he has by ſo many irrefragable proofs declared that he has ſent. Now upon all that hear me, and particularly upon thoſe who regulate their literary purſuits according to this plan, *peace be upon them, and upon the Iſrael of God.*

SERMON V.

MATT. vii. 16.

Ye shall know them by their Fruits.

THIS criterion, laid down by our Saviour, of the characters of men individually, holds equally of them when united in society. The proof then of the truth of any religion, Christianity, for instance, is best established by its utility; and how a writer, engaged in such a subject as the Decline and Fall of the Roman Empire, could be blind to such a representation of it, which naturally resulted from his subject, is indeed astonishing, could it not be accounted for from the uncommon vanity which seems to have accompanied him throughout, and from a desire of rendering his work agreeable to the depraved taste of the generality, rather than to that of the good and judicious. In the body of his work we are presented with a concise, yet laborious summary

summary of the Roman law, from which we necessarily infer the prodigious erudition of the writer; but it had certainly tended more to the enlightening of the reader, had each particular law, under the several general heads, been accompanied with the date when it was enacted, at least during the period that coincided with his work. In that case the laws had attested the history, and the history the laws, by shewing the reason and occasion of their promulgation. And then it may be conjectured, that, instead of seeming objections against Christianity, many considerations had been suggested in its favour, all tending to advance virtue, to improve manners, and consequently to increase the general stock of happiness among mankind.

Together with other advantages, it would have appeared that Christianity had introduced a more liberal law of nations. The Roman policy of constantly supporting the weaker against the stronger, the more effectually in the end to subdue both, was directly contrary to the spirit of Christianity, which has been known to interfere between the victor and the vanquished, moderating the extravagance of the one, and availing itself of every possible plea in favour of the other: nay, the Roman

Roman Prelates themselves, even in the worst times of the hierarchy, it must be owned, have often, where their peculiar interests were not concerned, shewn themselves the patrons of justice, the defenders of the distressed, and the gracious ministers of mercy. They have been known to protect, by threatening the aggressors with the terrible thunders of excommunication, the weaker and oppressed, against the stronger and encroaching nation, to summon to the tribunal of reason the claims of contending monarchs, and to determine, by their authority, in favour of the more equitable cause. The propagation of Christianity among the northern nations of Europe, through the aid derived to it from the newly-created emperors of the West, was indeed marked with violence. Those champions of the faith, marched as it were with the sword in one hand and the Scriptures in the other, the consequence was, that the vanquished were obliged to submit as well to the sovereignty, as to embrace the religion of their conquerors: perhaps these rude nations could not otherwise be brought under its light and easy yoke. Of this, since the increasing rays of science have illumined them, they are at last convinced.

vinced. Inclination has reconciled them to what neceffity introduced; and they cannot be infenfible of advantages which, however communicated, it is infinitely better to poffefs, than to be entirely deftitute of them.

Chriftianity has been by its divine Author compared to leaven: as that pervades the whole lump, fo is the former in a way to accomplifh its intended effect, the moral improvement and reformation of the world; but though, in conformity to the defigns of Providence, obftacles flowly recede, and more extenfive acceptance is as flowly obtained, yet evils which have been long in removing are lefs likely to return, and advantages not fuddenly attained are on that account the more prized, and confequently are of longer continuance. When Emperors fat on the throne to decide upon metaphyfical queftions, and oppofite parties in the ftate took different fides, the queftions at leaft were thoroughly agitated, and the learning of the age was rather increafed than otherwife: but if, under the immediate view of fuch authority, the abfolute determination of them was in vain attempted, the refult muft be to call our attention to more ufeful fpeculations, and to revive

the

SERMON V.

the genuine spirit of our religion, which consists less *in the knowledge that puffeth up, than in the charity that edifieth.*

A candid and legitimate historian of the Decline and Fall of the Roman Empire, had found a signal opportunity for displaying the merits of Christianity, as well in the duties of mercy and compassion that it generally recommends, as in its particularly discouraging those sanguinary sports, to which the antient Romans were so long habituated, and so fondly attached. If the then most polished nations were thus brutal in their pleasures, those destitute of their advantages must have been even more so. The suppression therefore of so popular and favourite an entertainment, could be attributed to nothing but to the effect of that mild and humane religion which had taken root, and spread wide its branches amongst them, at the time these amusements were entirely discontinued. That men should be trained to reciprocal ferocity, should for hire either receive or inflict wounds, and gain applause in proportion to their encountering danger with less fear, and as they endured the fatal stroke with greater resolution, to those educated in Christian sentiments seems astonishing: indeed nothing can be more so, except

cept that there should have existed human beings, and those pretending to high degrees of refinement, who were capable of deriving pleasure from so disgusting a spectacle. The contentions of the *blue and green* factions were frivolous indeed, often seditious; yet, when considered as superseding the shews of gladiators, their being afterwards exclusively encouraged may be regarded as an improvement introduced by Christianity, thus weaning men from sanguinary sports, and engaging them in those of mere amusement; not so useful as the scenes of the serious drama, which it encouraged, or indeed did not disapprove, as they tended to the purifying of the passions by holding up a faithful mirror to life, and by enriching with moral sentiments the human mind.

The mitigation of the penal laws might also have been, by an unprejudiced historian, numbered among the many advantages which the Empire received from the establishment of Christianity. The mutilated statues, dug from the remains of ruined cities, were supposed to be rendered thus by the hand of time; but further experience has clearly ascertained that they but too faithfully represent the horrid punishment usually inflicted on slaves or captives.

SERMON V.

tives. Surely even the fale of them was preferable to fuch a cruel treatment. Impaling, crucifixion, and other dreadful modes of execution, are now grown obfolete: while atrocious crimes are committed, capital punifhments will be neceffary; yet even where life is juftly forfeited, the laws fhould be content with depriving the guilty of it in a manner as little as poffible offenfive to the feelings of the fpectators, and not unneceffarily excruciating to thofe who fuffer. The cuftom of caufing criminals to look ftedfaftly on burning brafs till their fight was extinguifhed by it; a punifhment undoubtedly cruel, yet not equal to the abfolute deftruction of them; the configning to a monaftery, or to the office of the priefthood, which could not afterwards be refigned, thofe whofe crimes rendered them dangerous, or abilities fufpicious to the ftate; nay, the afylums afforded by religious inftitutions for offenders of all kinds, till the paffions of the injured fhould have time to cool; all feem to fpeak the efforts of Chriftianity to reconcile neceffity with indulgence, punifhment with mercy, and even the ftroke of death with an eafy infliction of it.

Our own age may be congratulated for being

ing infinitely lefs culpable in this refpect than thofe that have preceded it. The enormous cruelties that have accompanied the revolution in a neighbouring nation, have met in ours with almoft univerfal abhorrence: only a few excufed them as neceffary, to counteract their opponents, and therefore actually afcribable to *them*. But thofe who have been taught as the truth is in Jefus, never think themfelves juftified in returning evil for evil, but endeavour to overcome it with good; performing the latter at all events, and at the hazard of all confequences. Lately, too, when a Roman mode of punifhment was revived in a part of our ifland, ftill fubject to their laws, the affembled multitude turned away in difguft and deteftation of the horrid fight. Here then the manners as it were corrected the laws: and this conduct augured well, proving them in no fmall degree tinctured with the benevolent principles of our religion; and whatever legiflator fhall fo far comply with her fpirit as to expunge the too fanguinary pages that ftill difgrace our ftatute book, will deferve well of his country, of humanity; and at the fame time that he fhews by fuch an inftance how much he is concerned

for

for the dignity of human nature in general, he will afford an indisputable proof of the excellency of his own.

The author of the History of the Decline and Fall has occasion to remark the grossness of manners exhibited in common life by the antient Romans. Though represented to us, in their national character, as conquerors of the world, yet is there nothing amiable or engaging in their intercourse with each other as individuals: the insolence of the rich, the meanness of the poor, living upon offal regularly dispensed to them at the gates of the higher citizens; the haughtiness of the patron towards his client, even when he condescended to admit him to the same table; are quite foreign to modern opinions and practice. And to what is this owing but to Christianity, which summons to a tribunal before which the highest must bend, and which neglects not the claims of the very lowest? The doctrine, peculiarly its own, of charity, introduces the true and only practicable idea of equality, by which the wants of the many are relieved by the superfluities of the few; and its injunction, that the disciples *should wash one another's feet*, affords a question, whether it im-

prove

prove moſt thoſe who perform the duty, or thoſe to whom it is performed?

Hence condeſcenſion in ſuperiors, and ſubmiſſion from inferiors; hence the endearing offices of civility, courteſy, humanity; hence a participation in the pleaſures, as well as a ſenſe of the ſorrows of others; hence too we increaſe our own joys by communicating them, and derive comfort under our ſufferings from the pity and compaſſion which they excite. Hence our cities become ſocial and agreeable habitations, and our ſtreets are free from offence or violence; our couches too are ſecure from ſuſpicion or injury, and, inſtead of the ſolitude and drearineſs that reigns in the dens of ſavages, our tables afford occaſion for amuſement and inſtruction, for the effuſions of the underſtanding, or for the infinitely more valuable expanſions of the heart. Theſe advantages were ſeldom to any extent experienced before the eſtabliſhment of Chriſtianity; and that they are now ſo generally felt, muſt be reckoned among its moſt obvious and pleaſing effects.

The hiſtorian of the Decline and Fall is not to be blamed for not mentioning the influence of Chriſtianity on the laws which he has occaſion

casion to introduce. No; but the fault lies here, that he allows it not in this particular its full force. The severe edicts published by the Christian Emperors against adultery, speak them suggested by a system that requires the most exact and scrupulous purity of manners. The extremes to which this doctrine was carried were natural to a new tenet; and had our author been as desirous of selecting good, as he is of exposing depraved female characters, he might have found, even amongst the Empresses, such as were not less exemplary than they were elevated, who were shining instances of virtue and piety, and for the forming of whom the world was indebted to Christian principles.

The Roman law originally invested the husband with the same power over the wife that a father had over his son; namely, that of life and death. Divorces were likewise easily permitted, notwithstanding the frequent exertions of Christianity to regulate the institution according to our Saviour's plan, and to confine the causes of separation to those laid down in the Gospel: but Justinian, according to our author, consulted in his famous code the unbelieving Civilians, and his matrimonial laws, all owing in this respect greater indulgence,

gence, are influenced by the earthly motives of juſtice, policy, and the natural freedom of both ſexes. Happy times! in which, for the improvement of their morals, the works of ſuch writers are entruſted to the hands of youth. Surely that ſex will no longer be partial to an author, whoſe licentiouſneſs, in the pure times of the republic had been offenſive even to the dignity of a Roman matron, and who would deprive Chriſtianity of its boaſted pre-eminence, that of advancing, on the ſureſt grounds, the female character to its higheſt perfection.

It will be needleſs to mention, among other effects which the Romans, and ourſelves after them, have obtained by embracing Chriſtianity, the total abolition of the horrid cuſtom of human ſacrifices. Oroſius taxes them with it even in the glorious æra of their republic; and moreover tells them, in commendation of the Goſpel, that though it could not avert misfortunes, it furniſhed, however, the moſt effectual motives for enduring them. Yet there is a point, which, on the preſent ſubject, cannot but be mentioned, and which, by preventing human miſery in the extreme, has proportionally contributed to our happineſs; namely, the entire diſcouragement it ſhows to the

the before too prevalent cuſtom of ſuicide. It was that in which Stoiciſm principally prided itſelf; its lawfulneſs or unlawfulneſs was left undetermined by moſt of the other ſects; it was the fancied refuge too often ſought by weak, unenlightened, deſpairing nature; yet how little beneficial was it to the ſufferer, how fraught with terror to the ſurvivor?

But the doctrines of Chriſtianity naturally tend to reſtrain and compoſe the paſſions; and the conſiderations it ſuggeſts, of themſelves reſiſt and prevent this horrid practice. They teach, that, if we ſuffer for our ſins, it is but juſt that we ſhould abide by ſuch conſequences as we have brought upon ourſelves; that if we are oppreſſed by the divine vengeance, the ſatisfying of his juſtice here, is preferable to enduring the eternal effects of it hereafter: all impatience, diſtruſt, deſpair vaniſh before the idea of an omnipotent, yet all-gracious Being, who *can ſuccour us in all ſorrows*, and *deliver us from all dangers*, and *who in the midſt of wrath thinketh upon mercy*.

Another advantage, unqueſtionably to be attributed to Chriſtianity, and which this declamatory writer had ſuch an obvious opportunity of remarking, was the ſilence of the Oracles,

Oracles, which took place almost immediately on its establishment. When the real truth appeared, the fabrications of falsehood in course were mute; for that they were fallacious engines of deception, we at this time cannot doubt. Yet how long did they terrify and enthrall antient Greece, the nurse of science and of the arts; and, as if the imposition had not profited enough from human ignorance and credulity, the Romans adopted and continued it; whilst none of the boasted sages and philosophers of either nation was so kind as to open their eyes upon this subject. Socrates dared not do it, and Cicero, all-accomplished as he was, rather straitened than loosened the bands of this inveterate superstition.

Another, and still more glorious effect of Christianity, passed over with equal inattention by our author, is the total and complete overthrow of idolatry, atchieved in the period of which he treats, and which happened seemingly to his infinite regret. Yet what tongue can tell the immoralities of that mode of religion, what fancy but must be vitiated by its licentiousness, what conscience but must be harrowed up by the atrocities that accompanied it? The mere worshippers of the idol had

had been rightly enough left to the confequences of their weakness and folly; but it was to rescue those who were disgusted with the wickedness that was associated with such rites, that a revelation was, in the early ages of the world, vouchsafed from heaven: at first severe indeed in proportion to the obstinacy of the disorder intended to be remedied by it, but which in time was to yield to a milder dispensation, as more congenial to the infinite mercy of God. How misapplied then the talents, that could counteract so gracious a design! Our author therefore may be commended for brilliancy of style, may be proposed as a pattern of indefatigable industry, and of the most profound erudition, but none that is duly zealous of the dignity of human nature, but must abhor the design of apologising for a religion of such indelible infamy and debasement, as is idolatry; and he must equally reprobate the attempt (when the subject naturally led to the direct contrary) of calumniating the Christian institution, which, after the former had been rivetted for many ages among the customs of mankind, was, under God, the happy means of rescuing them from it.

[g] What a triumph did Christianity at last exhibit in the temple of Jupiter Ammon, in the city of the African Alexandria! The superb idol was erected in a temple, for grandeur and sublimity worthy of a metropolis, only next to the two capitols of the eastern and western world; in wealth, perhaps their superior. A pedestal supported it, in heighth above the ordinary human stature; but neither the pomp of the place, nor the enraged countenances of its numerous votaries, could abash the enterprising zeal of a band of determined Christians, collected for the purpose, who concluded an harangue against the folly and impiety of such a religion, by aiming, at the hazard of their lives, with such weapons as the present moment supplied, at the interior limbs of the stupendous statue a decisive blow. It came down with a tremendous thundering crash: the astonished multitude supposed the universe itself would have fallen with it; they paused awhile in silent and alarmed expectation, but as neither sun nor star, nor even the

---

[g] Le Beau Hist. du bas Empire, V. v. p. p. 342. He inserts a remarkable circumstance. On abbattit la tête, dont il sortoit une multitude de rats, auxquels ce Dieu servoit de retraite.

most insignificant object in the inanimate creation seemed affected by the event, the light of sense, of reason, of reflection, in an instant pierced the accumulated gloom, with which they had been from their infancy enveloped; and they treated their once adored divinity with indignity as extravagant as had been their former adoration. Thus, in about the two thousand five hundredth year of the world, was it at last, with some difficulty indeed, restored to the use of its senses. Go now, and boast of the omnipotence of human reason, doubt, if you can, of the necessity of a dispensation of grace, or question the power of revelation to guide, control, enlighten the human mind, and still admire such writers, who, though promising you liberty, yet are themselves the servants of corruption, which, should they communicate, the consequence must be, that you will be plunged into errors and enormities perhaps as debasing as idolatry itself.

The papistical modern writers, historians they would be thought, suppose, that, at the first separation of these kingdoms from the Church of Rome, the sacrifice of a few obnoxious tenets, on the part of the latter, had still retained the former in their accustomed obedience to the Holy See; but light once

let

let in upon a few of their diftinguifhing doctrines, muft have evinced the abfurdity of all the reft. So it has happened; and though one of their [b] writers, when treating on a fubject that naturally leads to it, omits the circumftance, yet it is manifeft, that the tenacioufnefs of the Latins in favour of image-worfhip, was the principal obftacle to their union with the Greek Church. Indeed the fpiritual flavery of thefe kingdoms had been but half removed, if, when the fupremacy of the Bifhop of Rome had been denied, the fervice in an unknown tongue, auricular confeffion, and image-worfhip, with all its train of follies, had been retained; and in the prefent enlightened ftate of the human mind, that fuch a corrupt mode of worfhip ftill continues, can only be attributed to the prevailing opinion, that Chriftianity, even under fuch a deformed appearance, is ftill infinitely preferable to the entire expulfion of it.

And we have an opportunity of obferving the truth of thefe remarks, and the effects of Chriftianity being extirpated, in the melancholy events lately fo frequent in the world around us; where the mifery arifing from its

[b] Church and State.

absence is more than can be expressed, and the distress nearly without remedy. But these dangerous innovations are particularly deprived of the advantages pointed out in this discourse, as immediately resulting from religion. Perhaps divine Providence intended that the moral effects produced by revelation, should in its later progress be as unequivocal arguments of its truth, as the suspension of nature's laws were at its commencement: if so, then the different effect of Christianity on human conduct, and that of the novel schemes, should as naturally determine your judgment, as the fire that descended from heaven at the command of Elijah, which the Priests of Baal, though challenged to it, could not perform, unalterably convinced the understandings of the Israelites. It is a continued series of such proofs that results from the facts recorded in general history, for the neglect or misrepresentation of which we have ventured to blame the writer of the History of the Decline and Fall of the Roman Empire, and it is the criterion to which, in conclusion, it is intended to refer you. If you think the atrocities occasioned by the authors of the late revolution sufficiently engaging to induce you to imitation, bid adieu to Christianity, and follow them; but if the mild virtues, and extensive blessings of society, produced by the doctrines of Christ, as imperfectly sketched out in this discourse, evidently declare him a teacher sent from God, then immediately, and at all events still continue *to follow him.*

SERMON VI.

JOHN xix. 11.

Jesus answered, Thou couldest have no power at all against me, unless it were given thee from above.

SO spoke the meek Jesus to the insolent Roman governor; the former, certainly in his person concentrating as it were all spiritual, the latter, representing in his the most extensive temporal power. The event which the text records, seems to describe the nature of both: in Christ the power was indisputably divine, to Pilate, according to our Saviour's own assertion, it was given from above. Whether temporal, then, or spiritual, they are alike derived from the same source: though the latter bears more uniform marks of its origin than the former, they are consequently compatible, and not, as is now the fashion to represent

present them, entirely inconsistent with each other. That they should always coincide, is no more than could be wished; but that the temporal should pursue its prescribed ends, the praise of the good, and the punishment of the wicked, is never so likely as when it associates with the spiritual. Even states unenlightened by revelation have seen the necessity of some kind of religion or other, and therefore have coalesced with false, rather than none; otherwise their stay and spring, as it were, had been languid and lost. For it is tyranny only that extorts obedience by severity, but judicious legislatures distinguish themselves as such by abrogating gradually, and as they can, sanguinary statutes; and by introducing such dispositions, as would in time, were they to become general, render all laws unnecessary. Intended to restrain the bad, they are by no means made for the good; and men are naturally rendered such by practising the precepts of that religion which most refines and purifies the mind, and places their affections on *things above, and not on things on the earth*. Wise states therefore naturally avail themselves of such principles; without which all absolute duties would want a necessary support, and all relative would become a

rope

rope of sand. It is true, laws cannot arraign the thoughts, as the words and actions, but this is because they cannot know them, otherwise *they* are as proper objects for their animadversion as the overt act; nay, wherever the intention is discerned, it either aggravates or mitigates the malignity of the offence. We are told, that with the salvation of the soul human governments have no concern: with the mind they certainly have; else why did so many sage nations of antiquity prescribe an education of their youth, correspondent to their several polities? It is certain, that if the virtues which all good laws enjoin do not actually *save* the soul, still they, in an eminent degree, contribute to it. The powers then that be, are ordained of God, as all truly spiritual are, and all falsely so, pretend to be; it follows that there is no absurdity in their coalescing, but that there thus exists a natural ground for their union, alliance, and harmony.

Our Saviour, the Lord of all things, yet acknowledges in the text the heaven-descended power of Pilate, and accordingly submits to it; pleads to the accusation, nor pretends to appeal from the decision of the tribunal. Indeed, whatever is received, must be so according

ing to the circumstances of the receiver. Christ, as a man, was subject to an human judicature: the spiritual powers, as they are called, though primarily derived from him, yet, as exercised by men, must be subject to it likewise—the Priest, the Prelate, the Apostle must yield to the pressure of human power. Even at present their extraordinary commission cannot exempt them from obeying the calls of ordinary prudence; being, as mortals, incompetent to secure every desirable end, they must therefore rest satisfied with those that are actually attainable, and, upon comparison of them, must often sacrifice the less advantageous to the more so---nay, submit to inferior, to avoid superior evils. The Church, while on earth, is militant, not triumphant, advancing towards, but not having yet attained perfection; its general conduct therefore, particularly its spiritual powers, must be limited by its present condition.

It should seem then, even from our Saviour's celebrated defence almost immediately after the text, *my kingdom is not of this world*, that it was not his intention that the spiritual should aim at being superior to the temporal power; nay, should they be found in the same hands, they should be considered fidered as equally diftinct as if they were in the poffeffion of different perfons. For though fpiritual concerns muft be effected by temporal means, otherwife they could not be promoted by men, yet muft merely temporal interefts never be advanced by confiderations folely fpiritual. The latter confer no more title to the former, than what would be valid without them: fpiritual power likewife trenches not on temporal rights, whether in a fupreme or fubordinate member of fociety.

It is indeed a lamentable circumftance, when the temporal oppofes the fpiritual power; particularly when it regulates not its decrees by reafon and juftice. True, the voice of law, wherever it refides, muft be obeyed; but if its declarations be fubverfive of generally acknowledged duties, or fhould it prepofteroufly countenance degrading and deftructive vices, though an outward obedience might be paid to it, yet will it not fail of exciting inward repugnance. No; the ftatutes of any nation may enjoin things indifferent to religion, but if they contradict or oppofe it, a ready and fincere obedience will fcarcely be paid to them.

And can fpiritual power ever control or oppofe the dictates of right reafon, or fufpend the

the practice of the duties enjoined by that very revelation from which it would be supposed to derive its authority? Really spiritual power cannot, but fictitious may. Such has been known to dispense with the most sacred engagements, to commit unjust violations of property, and to plead divine authority for the perpetration of the most horrid atrocities, to keep, *for merely human ends*, both body and soul under the most oppressive vassalage, and to exceed, in the severity of the torments they inflicted, the most sanguinary examples ever exhibited by temporal tribunals.

It were easy to illustrate this, from the history of, and measures pursued by, the Romish Church; but nowhere more apparently than in the annals of our own nation, as they coincide with those of what are commonly called the middle ages. This was a period in which we, as well as almost all Europe, were under deplorable bondage to the Holy See; a period that has employed the pen of a noble author now no more, and of a Roman Catholic writer at present living. The latter blames the former, and endeavours to undermine his well-earned reputation, even when he would appear most to praise him. Indeed to obliterate the impressions justly conveyed by that valuable

valuable work, seems one principal reason for the latter publication; and, probably for a similar purpose, the author of the Decline and Fall of the Roman Empire labours, in a posthumous production, to depreciate a work which, as far as it goes, is superior to his own. Suffice it however to observe, that, while alive, the noble Historian was but another name for Virtue, and it augurs ill for any cause, that it opens with an attack upon acknowledged merit; nay, what may be supposed the especial object of that writer, is rather impeded than promoted by it.

For, unfortunately, how little suited to vindicate the character of the Roman Catholic religion, is the period he has chosen for the subject of his history. It was the period when the schism in the Christian world was occasioned by there existing two infallible Bishops of Rome at once[1], the successors of the Fisherman, treading upon the necks of Kings—when the joys of heaven were promised as motives to ensure obedience to the commands of the Papacy, while the pains of hell were denounced against such as would not leave their country, their fortune, their

---

[1] Alexander and Victor.

family,

family, for the vain purpose of rescuing the holy sepulchre from the hands of Infidels—when the proud, bigotted, and ungrateful Becket, flew from the authority of his liege Lord, and sheltering himself under that of a foreign Prince, defended what he called his spiritual rights, which were indeed no other than ecclesiastical usurpations, forced from the reluctant hands of the immediately preceding monarchs—when, after the recent conquest of the kingdom, favours were to be liberally dispensed, and the powerful Churchmen were, at all events, to be reconciled to the victor, or, when rival claimants of the Crown afforded an opportunity to the ambitious, of selling at the highest price their assistance; the struggles of virtue and reason were then unable to resist such encroachments as those, which, if after ages had suffered them to remain, we should at this time have had neither science nor liberty.

[k] The dreadful vengeance then taken on such well-meant attempts in the persons of the Albigenses, whose miseries were more terrible than all that antient history records, and these inflicted immediately by, or at the sug-

---

[k] Vide Berrington's History of Henry II. p. 515.

gestions of a common parent, who only meant, it seems, by such hard treatment, to correct, console, convert them (yet these innocent victims suffered for no other opinions, than what the Reformation afterwards proved both rational and tenable): all these instances demonstrate this period most of all others pregnant with papistical encroachments. It was then in the full exertion of its most extravagant pretensions to power, and then exhibited the most glaring examples of the abuse of it, as they have indeed been generally esteemed by such as have been best qualified to judge of them. The attempt therefore to represent this era as conducive to the reputation of Roman Catholicism, is not only novel, but betrays as great a degree of caprice as of obstinacy.

But this is the age of novelties. Formerly the arguments of Protestantism were attested by the best Roman Catholic writers: Erasmus, Muratori, Thuanus, Giannoni, are as loud in execrating the abuses of the See, falsely called Holy, as the most zealous Protestants; nor do they screen its insatiableness, its impurity, its tyranny, its total inconsistency with civil and religious liberty, its entire want of support either in common sense or sound learning. Far different the purposes of the writer at present considered, who prolongs his history two reigns beyond that of the noble author before mentioned, with this view (and an extraordinary one it is), that he may represent the tendency of the Roman Catholic religion, to advance the purposes of civil and religious liberty. Indeed when the whole realm consisted of Catholics, what merit they, as such, could derive from exertions in its cause, is not easily imagined; and when homage was performed by our own Monarch, to a foreign ecclesiastical potentate, for the crown of these kingdoms, its political liberty seems not much to have been promoted. But homage, it seems, was a mere formality, an happy expedient to secure one state from the depredations with which it was threatened by another: while under the sheltering wing of the Church, invaders dared not assault it; and, the danger past, the protected might retire again, without loss or injury as to right, power, and property.* So thought not the politic monarchs of these days: they never swore fealty to another, unless he had an indisputable right, or unless they were forcibly

---

* Vide Berrington's History of Henry II. p. 596. He calls it a nominal evil, which we could cast off at pleasure.

compelled to it.[1] The arts too of the Romish See were too well known, for any to trust it farther than could be avoided. Its most favourite and nearest Royal sons would not suffer any of its decrees to have the force of laws in their dominions, without a previous examination, and an express licence to that purpose. These spiritual monarchs, too, were the more dangerous, inasmuch as the life of a single individual is too short for any vast schemes of ambition; but an ecclesiastical state, always existing, can supply the deficiency of one of its heads by the expertness of his successor, is contemporary with the longest plan, and is sure to avail itself, in the end, of the infirmity or inability of those who, in the course of time, might rise to oppose it. So thought the most enlightened and nearest princes even in professed subjection to the Court of Rome.

They therefore regarded with reluctance her advances towards immoderate power, opposed, and sometimes successfully impeded them; nay, often supported one head of the Church against another, besieged the reigning pontif even in Rome itself, and more than

---

[1] It was called the Exæquatur regium. Vide Giannoni Istoria di Napoli, Vol. IV. p. 204.

once expelled him from it, and very deservedly; for they who served him most, were always sure of being the least rewarded. Spirited and resolute kings they dreaded, but weak and wicked ones they effectually subdued to their purposes, by absolving subjects from their oath of allegiance, by laying whole kingdoms under an interdict, or threatening them with the more dreadful sentence of excommunication.

^m For this affected civil as well as spiritual rights: subjects were liable to it, not for their own faults, but for those of their Sovereigns. Instead of merely abstaining from the society of one under that sentence (which was the only idea of excommunication appointed by the Apostles), the unhappy sufferers could neither acquire nor possess any increase of property: the physician would scarcely approach him, his testimony was rejected in a court of justice, he could sue for no debts, accept no legacy, nor insist upon the performance of any agreement; and in case of death, his last testament was deprived of validity. After so many glaring instances (and history is full of the records of such tyranny exercised by the

---

^m See also Berrington's History of Henry II. p. 163.

Romish

Romish Church), shall we be any longer told of its essential tendency to favour liberty?

The obtaining of the great charter in the time of King John, was indeed a signal triumph in its cause; and this our author vauntingly attributes to the Roman Catholics at that time: however, as has been already observed, the whole nation was so; they therefore, as such, could derive but little merit from it. But for whom was it obtained? For the nobility, the knights, and higher order of the clergy: its benefits extended not to the lower orders, who notwithstanding continued, like the cattle, to be transferred from one occupier to another; nay, one article of the charter expressly secures to the master the possession of such kind of property. Its influence too was almost as soon suspended as obtained. Resolute and enterprising princes succeeded to the crown of these realms, as regardless of the rights of their subjects, as of the threats of the See of Rome; and it was not till more modern times, that the effects of the grand charter were revived in that brighter display of liberty, which the Revolution has given us to enjoy.

And it was an attainment with difficulty acquired, and which, therefore, cannot be too highly

highly prized; but it has been accompanied with such alarming abuses, so many have perverted it to base purposes, that, as in religion, so with respect to liberty, those that pretend to most, have generally the least regard for either. It is then most desirable, when its comforts are inwardly felt, and its benefits outwardly experienced; " not when we are " told we want it," otherwise we should not have known it: this, whether lost or acquired, can very little influence our happiness. It was of the former kind, that the noble author just mentioned was the able and strenuous advocate, and he could reconcile being so with a justly conceived [n] *horror of popery:* but what kind of liberty that must be which his antagonist can reconcile with a professed love for that corrupt and tyrannical form of religion, may be left to the determination of the impartial.

To their decision, likewise, we may submit the question, which of the two writers is the most consistent: but to what shall we attribute the hatred of the latter to state-religions, as he contemptuously calls them? Are they incompatible with liberty? or are they essen-

[n] Vide Preface to Berrington's History of Henry II. p. 21.

tially

tially different from the establishment of the Roman Catholic Church? If state-religions are inconsistent with liberty, how comes the author to belong to one? for surely such is that of Rome; and if she alone is favourable to liberty, how came her ordinary measures so repugnant to it? The state reaps this advantage from coalescing with religion, that they become reciprocally checks upon each other. Those who possess spiritual rights, must needs be subject to those endued with temporal power, that they may be a restraint upon them, lest their conduct should be unworthy of the divine commission with which they are entrusted; and kings themselves must be improved, from having the Gospel truths regularly suggested to them. Hence their subjects of all ranks are rendered the happier, by the effect of such gentle, yet efficacious interference. But the papal power, after arrogating to itself authority both spiritual and temporal, proceeded so far, as to endeavour to secure her own encroachments, by encouraging avaricious monarchs in their depredations on their subjects and others: nay, there is one instance on record, of one pontif, who proposed to revive obsolete claims on the subjects of a neighbouring king°, and, to induce him to countenance them, offered to share with him the profits. But even he, though a prince by no means inattentive to the calls of interest, yet could not but reject so infamous a proposal. Is there then any consistency in rendering the world indisposed to state-religions, capable of restraining both the contracting parties, and confining in some sort each to their duty, and, at the same time, in pretending to justify an establishment, where neither the temporal nor spiritual power is under any control; where assumed infallibility contradicts obvious truth, and where power pretending to be divine, and therefore implying perfection, is only conspicuous in producing the most alarming and extravagant abuses?

ᵖ The author boasts of the success of the Roman Catholic religion, in improving the laws. Alas! it encouraged single combat, the ordeal, and acquittal according to the majority of compurgators (the court of the Inquisition is purposely omitted, because that must close the argument at once, and more remains to be said); where the consideration

---

* Giannoni Istoria di Napoli.
ᵖ See Berrington's History of Henry II. p. 638.

SERMON VI.

of the real merits of a question was never attempted, nor wished to be introduced. The improvement in jurisprudence, attributed to Christianity in the last discourse, was principally owing to the Eastern, not the Western empire; Constantinople, not Rome, produced the Theodosian, Justinian, and afterwards the Basilian code. As to advancement in the arts, under the same religion, the specimens still surviving are exact, laboured, and minute, but are neither sublime, spirited, nor comprehensive [q]. In regard to the monks, too, though their merit might be unquestionable as copiers and preservers of manuscripts, yet ardour in collecting, diligence in multiplying, and liberality in communicating them, were wanting; nor even so did they atone for their indolence, insociability, and all the deformed train of monastic vices. Their very numbers, and various orders, spoke their corruption; for more had been unnecessary, had the first founded strictly adhered to their respective *rules*. They and literature, therefore, were of different interests: they accordingly rendered the dark ages still darker, till what re-

---

[q] See Appendix I. to Berrington's History of Henry II. p. 616, 617.

mained of antient art and letters, retiring from the siege of Constantinople by the Turks, at last took shelter in Italy, where it excited general and merited approbation, and happily coinciding with a desire of reformation, which the papal abuses had occasioned throughout the world, it contributed to those effects, which the ages since have experienced and admired. For nearly at one and the same time the operations of nature were more minutely investigated, our most holy religion revived, pure and refined from former taints and corruptions, and, by the application of the same accurate and extensive erudition, even the grounds of civil and political liberty were then first fully developed and explained.

What therefore this author attributes to the Roman Catholics, is in reality the appropriate praise of Protestantism. The truth is, the former did not only not communicate knowledge, but made the most unjustifiable use of the little it had, as it were, monopolized. While men are men, strong minds will influence weak ones; and though it ought not to be so, yet knowledge will generally avail itself of its powers to dupe and mislead the ignorant. Now what does this consideration, but point out the remedy for this
incon-

inconvenience, which is to endeavour to disseminate knowledge, and to place mankind as nearly as possible on a level in this respect? And this Protestantism has all along laboured to effect, though it is still contrary to the practice of the Romish Church; for to the former the laity are indebted not only that they can read, but that they have any thing to read. All the comfort and consolation derived from the holy Scriptures, are to be ascribed to the Reformation. This was a liberty with which the Romish Church had no notion of indulging ordinary Christians. Formerly the lowest of their Clergy in literary acquisitions were not much above the lowest of our present laity: now the middle ranks of the laity among us are capable of judging of the literary pretensions of the highest of their Clergy; and from the moderately, or even deeply learned, neither the cause of true religion, of our Church, or of even real liberty, has any thing to fear. It is from the partially learned, or, what is worse, from lettered wickedness, unduly influencing the well-disposed, but comparatively ignorant (and such the great mass of the people will generally be found), that our religion, as well as every

other

other important interest of humanity, has most to apprehend.

'The court of Rome had, and perhaps now has, an office for the licensing of such books as are supposed to be published under its authority. Through negligence, or corruption, or both, it has often happened that good books, not paying for the imprimatur, were prohibited, and bad ones, for which the permission had been purchased, were edited. Hence in states in communion with the Church of Rome, its imprimatur attracted no great veneration; and it became necessary, notwithstanding that recommendation, to revise such books ere they were suffered to be sold. We have run into the contrary extreme. With us, in the kingdom at large, all books are published, whether good or bad, without undergoing a previous examination; nay, such as, consistently with its practice, even the Church of Rome herself would not have suffered to be printed. No; she is too wise even implicitly to undermine her own establishment; and the mischief is, that they who live by writing regard not how much,

---

ʳ Vide Giannoni, p. 432.

but

but those who do not, care not how little they write. Yet it is incumbent on all who can, particularly to obviate the insidious tendency of such works as that of the author who has been considered in this discourse, that the writers themselves may not imagine they are practising thus unobserved upon the unwary; that plain men may not conceive, because *they* cannot readily answer a work replete with dangerous novelties, that therefore it is absolutely unanswerable; or that, because it receives not an immediate reply, it actually admits of none; and that the generality of Papists themselves may be made sensible of the inconsistency of those to whom, perhaps, they have entrusted the conduct of their consciences, and the guidance of their practice. To what consistency, for instance, can our author pretend, who is so far betrayed by his new passion for liberty, as to praise two individuals for things directly contrary to each other; namely, Stephen Langton and Thomas à Becket; the latter of whom supported the Roman pontif against the king— whereas the former opposed him through the king. If Becket was right, Langton was indisputably wrong; but if the saint was wrong, the cardinal was as certainly right. And whence

in

in this author such unseemly zeal against establishments, since every argument against them applies with equal force against the Church of Rome, of which, notwithstanding, he professes himself a faithful member, unless indeed his aim be first to destroy other religious establishments, and afterwards to erect the Roman upon their ruins; which will then take place, when men shall be inclined to substitute for what is, in most respects, good, that which is infinitely worse, in almost all views and considerations.

[s] Even the head of the latter Church, possessed, as he supposes himself, of powers eminently spiritual, is obliged, as his divine Master condescended to do in the text, to submit to necessity; which, like the power of the Roman governor, is at least permitted from above. Our author affirms, that our Saxon ancestors were as obedient to the Roman See as our Norman: it was however to that Church not yet corrupted and polluted, but only receptive of those seeds which afterwards sprung up in such rank luxuriance. Let it return to what it then was, and many pretensions in its

[s] Vide Berrington's History of Henry II. Appendix I. p. 525.

favour,

SERMON VI.

favour, as contained in the later history of our Henry the Second, would be acquiesced in. In ⁱ the time of Jansenism, the then reigning pontif only not consented to establish, as true, several propositions highly consonant to Protestantism: this had been done, had not apparently human necessity stepped in, and coerced, as usual, the supposed spiritual powers. The Jesuits, it seems, had at that time signally served the Roman See, in an interest that had to compromise with the state of Venice: *their* friendship therefore, and the establishment of the proposition could not stand together, as they were the determined supporters of the opinions of their brother Molina, against the Jansenists; so that, lest he might be taxed with ingratitude, the obnoxious decrees of the Trentine Council, though tottering to their fall, revived in all their pristine vigour and absurdity; and the so long expected propositions were never after heard of but in history. Lately, too, the head of the same Church condescended to accept of assistance from us, while we were able to afford it, who were before esteemed heretics and aliens. Why should not a similar necessity, that caused his

---

ⁱ Vide Catechisme du Jansenisme.

predecessor

predecessor to suspend a satisfactory measure, engage his successor[u] to renew it; at least he has nothing to fear from the scruples, in matters of religion, of the new ally lately forced upon him. Were something like this done, the desired consistency, as well in the head of that Church, as in those of its members who have lately renounced its most dangerous doctrines, might be obtained (for of the sincerity of the generality there can be no doubt); though some have wished to appear such violent partizans in the cause of liberty. New civil privileges might then be granted, in proportion as pure and genuine Christianity was restored. Instead of making a gain of subject nations, the really Catholic Church might be better employed in diffusing the conciliatory spirit of extensive charity and of universal benevolence, and the common faith would not have reason to number among its enemies those who profess to be most firmly attached to it. The pontif of Rome would have no more concern in the temporal interests of this country, than the primate of our Church has in those of Italy; yet both might, in their respective necessities, reciprocally assist each

[u] Buonaparte.

other;

other; nay, one golden chain of love, concord, harmony, might embrace the whole Christian world. Not only *nation would not rise up against nation*, but different churches would forget their contests, disputes, and dissensions, till they should in the end become, according to their original design, *one flock under one shepherd, Jesus Christ our Lord*.

SERMON VII.

Acts xxii. 28.

But I was free born.

IN the last discourse there was occasion to mention the two powers; the spiritual and the temporal. The present will require that the spiritual and the ecclesiastical should be distinguished from each other, and their limits duly ascertained. By spiritual power then is meant that with which men are invested by the supreme Being, or by Christ in obedience to him; by ecclesiastical, such as states and kings have condescended to confer on the church and its ministers: such as were certain privileges, somewhat similar to those on which St. Paul prides himself in the text, or certain species of property, with which, since the extensive adoption of Christianity, it has pleased the rulers of this world to endow, or even enrich it.

The former kind cannot, as it is said, be exercised but by those who, in regular succession, have been ordained to it; but this notion seems to have arisen more from prescription than from actual impossibility. Order, however, and decency, as well as obedience to custom, from the time of the Apostles, and conformity to the divine commission, actually delivered to the priesthood from our Saviour himself, require that a particular body of men should be generally separated to such sacred services; and though the apparently distinct powers are but species of that which was originally derived from above, and are consequently compatible, yet our sovereigns have wisely abstained from interfering with the spiritual, contenting themselves solely with the jurisdiction over the ecclesiastical state within their dominions.

If some of their pretensions seem to insinuate more than this, it is owing to the similar claims of the court of Rome. For though, at first view, it might be thought absurd to suppose a weak or wicked prince to be endued with spiritual powers, yet the popes were but men likewise, earthly potentates, excelling in refined policy and in extensive ambition—the most enterprizing of merely secular princes, and

and the worst kings that this nation has ever obeyed, might as safely have been trusted with divine powers, as many bishops of Rome that might be mentioned, or as many priests, who have unfortunately disgraced the common faith, and impiously perverted the purposes of their profession.

But there can be no objection to the ecclesiastical power, as already defined, residing in the supreme governor of a state; else he would be king over his subjects in one respect, and not so in another, and would find sophistry and sedition contrive so to confound temporal with spiritual claims, that by degrees his entire authority would be surreptitiously taken from him. Christ, it is true, declared, *that his kingdom was not of this world;* but it is of the invisible, not the visible, that he was then speaking; the latter, as consisting of men of all countries, conditions, qualities, and descriptions, he never could intend to withdraw from the power of the civil magistrate, otherwise the utmost discord and confusion had ensued. Nay, as just and equitable government is the design of Providence, the rule indeed to which he accommodates his own measures, there can be no impropriety, where the ends are the same, that the two powers, the temporal and the spiritual,

spiritual, should combine for the attainment of them. Again, as religion is the friend of rational liberty, nor subjects us to absurd restraint, there can be no reason why she should refuse such aid, defence, and even establishment, as the civil magistrate shall be inclined to bestow upon her. The Apostle in the text thought not that his sacred character exempted him from enjoying a civil privilege, the right of Roman citizenship; why then should not a number of individuals, when united in a society, in a church for instance, accept them, when they are offered, or may be otherwise obtained?

But " Christianity, it seems, flourished " many years without such aids. It was de- " rived at first from its divine Author per- " fect; human additions therefore are not " improvements, but incumbrances:" yet it has since flourished longer under them, than it did ere it had acquired them. Even the works of God are limited by the end to be promoted by them. If he intended his religion should, after a certain period, be actually thus supported, its authenticity cannot be disproved by its attaining that very advantage. If all that comes from God must be absolutely perfect, and admit of no improvement

or

or alteration, the Jewish dispensation must have still continued; nor could the Christian have succeeded it. The essential doctrines of the Gospel, indeed, remain the same to-day, yesterday, and for ever; but its accidental regulations depend upon times, places, and events, according to the different circumstances of the several states which have embraced it. Such of its institutions therefore are to be estimated, not by an imaginary idea of perfection, but as they coincide with such succeeding changes, and such continually recurring necessity.

The temporal power, though it might certainly subsist without the spiritual, yet it could not so effectually promote its best purposes when solitary, as when associated with it; but the latter could still less dispense with the aid afforded to it by the former. What pains and torments did the martyrs and first Christians undergo, merely because their religion was not professed by the temporal powers[w]! And though they thus gave the most indisputable proof of their sincerity, yet how much did it tend to its further propagation, that the kings of the earth afterwards assisted and sup-

[w] Vide Hooker, passim.

ported

ported it! There was as much propriety *then* in the prefence of fuch patronage, as there was before in its abfence. Miracles had ceafed, nothing remained to recommend it, but fuperior purity of morals in thofe who profeffed it, and the abfolutely fpiritual confiderations which it inculcated; all its other fources of authority were founded on the generofity and on the fupport it met with from thofe in whofe realms it was at length encouraged and embraced. As the Pagan priefts had all along appropriate revenues affigned to them, it feemed but natural that thofe of the true religion fhould not be in this refpect inferior to them. Frefh events called for frefh regulations, not afcribable to the genius of the Gofpel, but to continual errors and abufes arifing among thofe who profeffed it, till at length the evil proceeded fo far as to corrupt and fubvert the very effentials of religion, as well as to be highly injurious to the feveral political ftates which had hitherto fupported it: for the Roman prelates, inftead of refting fatisfied with being fubject to the temporal power, at length ufurped it, and, inftead of receiving as a favour a decent maintenance, appropriated to themfelves, under a pretence of promoting Chriftianity, royal revenues, and

fubftituted

SERMON VII.

substituted in support of their claims, for the mild methods of reason and persuasion, the more violent ones of force and persecution.

It was to confirm the benefits accruing from the establishment of Christianity, as well as to remedy the evils occasionally arising from it, that the Reformation gave birth to, and multiplied the regulations, that are at present in force in this kingdom with respect to it; wherefore then urge the inexpediency of these instances of reform, by pointing out the times when they were neither introduced nor known? The reason is, that the abuses which called for them, and to which they were subsequently applied, did not then exist; wherefore defend Roman Catholicism, because some of its now obnoxious doctrines were at first professed even by Protestants? For as Christianity itself did not immediately obtain general acceptance, so neither was the entire reformation of it immediately effected: all the further improvements and restrictions that have since been introduced for its protection and continuance, arose from the subsequent attempts to weaken, frustrate, and subvert it.

And if Christianity in general has need of temporal support, so especially, after its having been reformed, is such aid necessary; since

it

it has not only much to apprehend from vice, folly, and ignorance in general, but likewise from open or concealed enemies, who are even multiplied, from envy, at its being thus countenanced. Yet it cannot accept the advantage maliciously allowed it by its adversaries; namely, that it is permitted merely because it has the voice of the majority in its favour. This it would gladly procure and retain, yet it rests not its pretensions to preference on that ground solely; for its right to establishment would still remain the same, even were the majority against it. Nay, it is against the possibility of such a majority, that such guards and fences are necessary: and these it claims, as dependent on that general idea of law, the first prototype of which is the Deity himself[x]; which, though founded in reason, yet is still a restraint, and therefore not likely to engage the affections of the multitude; its principles besides are such as they would not consider, perhaps have not abilities to comprehend. Modes of worship, therefore, where men heap to themselves what teachers they will, or where absolution may be purchased for almost any crime, and where they may

[x] Vide Hooker, passim.

disburthen

disburthen their consciences by attending to a number of idle and frivolous ceremonies, are more likely to attract the regard of the majority, than those which require a generally accurate moral conduct, which profess to be directed by right reason, and propose no other means of procuring the divine favour, than the practice of pure and genuine piety [y]. Those too who allow them the voice of the majority, only intend to avail themselves of it when they shall, in their turn, have gained it on their side; and at which, it may be presumed, they aim, from their boasting of *millions* being of their opinion, and from the pains they take in making proselytes. But should they succeed, still the difference between Protestantism and other modes of religion will remain on the same basis as before; namely, superiority in reasoning, and preponderancy of argument.

But this venerated majority, where is it, or of whom does it consist? Could it be ascertained, or rendered more permanent, or in unison with itself, its decrees were certainly more binding and respectable; but fictitious majorities are here to-day and gone to-morrow; the succeeding have been often known

---

[y] Church and State.

to determine the direct contrary to the preceding; those that might be supposed to form a real and legitimate majority are too wise to suffer the truth or falsehood of their opinion to depend merely on its popularity, too modest to solicit abettors, or too well convinced to require the aid of numbers to give weight to a well-founded determination. How different the so much boasted of majorities, who are influenced not by the reasonableness of the measure, but by the good or ill success of it; who generally coincide in sentiment with the last speaker, the greater part of whom, like the Ephesian multitude, *know not wherefore they are gathered together*; whom cunning men mould and fashion to their own purposes, and that the more easily the more numerous they are! It is to remedy such inconveniences, that the best governments have, instead of those too ductile constituents, admitted to a share of power their representatives, who are often known, for their real interest and happiness, to determine the direct contrary to the biassed and prejudiced inclinations of their principals.

"We have, it seems, a parliamentary religion;

[z] Church and State, p. 542.

gion; not quite that—but an ecclesiastical establishment, sanctioned by the laws of the land, which our adversaries would fain have if they could; nay, they would entitle themselves to it by representing their religion as the only true one. Well, then, if they allow Christianity, as such, to have a claim to the support of the civil magistrate, upon that question we are fairly at issue; we will rest our pretensions to preference on the superior purity of Protestantism, on its comparatively greater correspondence with the Gospel in essential, and with reason and common sense in accidental circumstances.

But though we may assent to the proposition, that genuine religion may, and ought to be supported by the temporal power (indeed it is upon that ground only that we accept of aid for our own, which, as a branch of Protestantism, we shall not fail to assert to be a part of the really Christian Church); yet, after what has been said, it will hardly be expected that another popular opinion should be admitted as an axiom, that all [a] power is in the people. All force certainly is, should they unite in exerting it: the idea of power, how-

[a] Church and State, passim.

ever, suggests something of reason and equity; but when they boast of force exclusively, they seem to wave all other considerations. There is a difficulty, and that apparently insurmountable, in the idea of their being the centre of power, or rather of government [b]; namely, if they are so, to answer the question, who are the governed? It is said, that ours being a state-religion, what conferred upon us our provision can, if it pleases, resume it. Equally with that of other subjects; but this can in neither case be done with justice; for the preservation of property is one of the principal ends for which society was instituted; and whenever the state shall act so arbitrarily as to disregard it, we could not cheerfully acquiesce in such a step, though it were the will of the majority: we should therefore resist it by all legal methods: both our hearts and our pens would be engaged in restoring the legislature to a better mind; but we should not hypocritically own the justice of the sentence as thus decreed, and at the same time write against it.

Yet this is not the crime with which the Clergy of our Church are charged. No, they

[b] Church and State, p. 555.

are too much attached to government, as an image of that law and order which, though occafionally obfcured, yet primarily refide in the bofom of the Deity: not one in an hundred is a partizan of fedition, or even of oppofition. Much to our honour. We are enough convinced of the evil of party, ever in the leaft to countenance it. Peace we feek, peace we promote in our public and private provinces. We do not complain that the power of the fword is denied us; but our fincere prayer to God is, that all mankind would live together in unity and godly love. We teach no man, however wicked, to defpair of the divine mercy. Of the imperfections of all human inftitutions we are fufficiently apprifed, and charitably hope, while the effentials of the conftitution are preferved, that, whoever guides the helm, the fafety of the political veffel, even admitting occafional faults and errors, is not entirely to be defpaired of.

Notwithftanding the confidence of fome Roman Catholic writers, who would reprefent thofe of their profeffion as the actual champions in the caufe of civil and religious liberty, yet it was found, when there was a real neceffity for exertion, none were more ftrenuous

in

in their defence of it, than this our Proteſtant Clergy and Epiſcopacy. When the ᶜ ſage of the law lamented, that he had nearly ſurvived both that and the conſtitution, in conſequence of the tyrannical meaſures of a Popiſh king, directed by a Popiſh confeſſor, it was our ſacred band, that, uniting with a real and enlightened majority, took the lead in an event that revived and reſtored the injured rights of mankind, conferred honour on themſelves and on their lateſt poſterity, and ſhall for ever endear the Britiſh name to all lovers of rational religion, and of practical, becauſe duly limited liberty.

A decent warmth on this occaſion cannot be miſplaced, which has been excited by a book lately publiſhed, intitled, *Church and State*; a work, particularly at this time, of moſt dangerous tendency. It is not an hiſtory: indeed one knows not what to call it; except we ſay, that it boldly fills up the outline timidly traced by the Roman Catholic writer of the Hiſtory of Henry the Second. The principles in the body of the work are thoſe that have already been conſidered in this

---

ᶜ Serjeant Maynard.

diſcourſe:

discourse: omitting, therefore, his moſt curious account of [d] tythes (which, as he ſtates it, no law, as now explained by cuſtom, allows, neither are the Clergy ſo exorbitant as to demand them to ſuch an extent), his promptitude to charge others with bigotry, and ſuch offenſive appellations, his [e] ſhameful defamation of a learned Prelate [f], who in his time poſſeſſed a moſt extraordinary genius, and was generally right in his poſitions, though an argument or two might be ill-founded—proceed we, in the laſt place, principally to conſider the Appendix, which clearly diſcovers the deſign of the whole work, and which, had the learned object of our author's obloquy ſtill ſurvived, had afforded an ample field for the exerciſe of the talent in which he particularly excelled; namely, that of detecting inconſiſtencies. Indeed to one at all converſant in our hiſtory, it muſt appear ſtrange, that, after the enemies of our eſtabliſhment had all along continued to tax it with a ſtill too cloſe imitation of Popery, it ſhould at laſt be diſcovered that they and the Roman Catholics meant the ſame thing, were equally enemies to ſtate-religions, or, which is much the ſame, were

---

[d] Church and State, p. 323.   [e] Ibid. p. 411.
[f] Biſhop Warburton.

equally

equally desirous of supplanting that which boasts itself, though not exclusively, to be the true one. All this appeared mysterious, till the Appendix resolved the difficulty, by declaring the Roman Catholic religion a friend to a party, too ludicrous to be mentioned in a serious discourse, formerly respectable indeed, but now by some esteemed as no better than another name for sedition. It is not at present easy to perceive how it can be an objection to one mode of religion, that it is established, and at the same time a recommendation to another, that it naturally connects itself with a popular party. But the true Christian is of none; his aim is to promote the good of his country, or rather of all mankind; which can never happen through the subversion of religion, now, alas! too much to be apprehended, unless its present dangers should call down fresh aids from above. But no wonder a party-man should extol the decision of the multitude, since it is the very seal and token of such associations, that a man renounces his private reason and opinion to obey the determination of the majority; this being the only way of forcing the party into notice or consequence.

With what an ill grace, then, does the charge

charge of *temporizing* proceed from the pen of such a writer, which is, as he defines it, complying with the prevailing opinion, though contrary to a man's own, for the sake of present emolument; as if the Prelates of Rome never temporized. He stigmatizes with this charge an 'eminent Protestant writer, now living, who certainly merits it not either from him or any other Roman Catholic, since his literary labours have been principally employed, and successfully too, in vindicating the character of an unfortunate princess of that persuasion, and in exposing the arts of her malicious rival, in procuring her destruction; an act which no policy can justify, no words can palliate. He condemns the party rage so violent at the commencement of the present century, when he says the groundless alarm was excited of the Church being in danger; as if the one at present propagated, of the subject's liberty being in similar peril, was not equally the artifice of the same spirit. Daring encroachments produce strong measures; and when we cannot traverse our streets, travel on our public roads, or rest in our beds in safety, from the excesses of an ill-regulated freedom,

---

g Whitaker. Vide Church and State, notes, p. 581.

the consequence is much the same as if we were under the most inexorable tyranny. And to what is this owing, but to that phrensy of the multitude, which, as an excellent author observes, is so unaccountably and invariably converted to the benefit of the few? [g] He apologizes, as a lawyer, for meddling with theology: it is a general concern, and therefore no excuse is necessary: but his strictures in the body of the book, on our Articles, are certainly out of his province; it is a matter between the subscriber to them, and his conscience. Here, therefore, an apology had been decorous; perhaps it had been more so, to have omitted the observations altogether.

[h] The opinion of our author, and the one considered in the former discourse, are somewhat different with respect to the Inquisition: the latter fairly gives it up, as inconsistent with the reputation of any government, and a disgrace to any religion; the former, though he condemns it, yet lays the blame even of that institution still upon a state-religion. This is the phantom that haunts him, the cause of every ill; and its removal, as he thinks, would be attended with that of every other calamity:

---

[h] Church and State, p. 381.   [i] Ibid. p. 609.

as

as if, with respect to a bad measure, the question was, who was subject to it, not who invented, suggested, encouraged it. The magnanimity of the English Roman Catholics is extolled, as if they, exclusively of other subjects, resisted its introduction into these kingdoms. Alas! they had no power to prevent it; but it was contrary to the principles of our constitution, either in Church or State, to endure the very name of it. Had it depended upon them, they must, consistently with the genius of their religion, like many other nations in communion with the See of Rome, have bowed their necks to this galling and tormenting yoke.

Thus much for this author, and for, as he thinks it, his unanswerable work; the alarming danger to be apprehended from which must apologize for its having detained us so long. For a single wicked act and its consequences end when the perpetrator has satisfied that justice which he has provoked; but wicked principles are perpetually productive: against them the sword of the magistrate is drawn in vain; and when inveterate, the pen of the writer, or voice of the preacher, are often ineffectually employed to suppress them.

them. But this age has seen not only principles separately directed to the ruin of our common faith, but jointly and systematically contributing their efforts to that purpose. The scheme has been a long while formed, or there never were such manifest signs of its having been so: the springs of moral science, as contained in general history and in the Scripture, are tainted and corrupted. Voltaire began with exposing to ridicule the most sacred subjects; Priestley followed, and by mutilation and interpolation attempted to overturn the doctrine of the soul's immortality, and to banish all mystery from revelation; furnishing a specimen how the Scripture might be made to support any tenet or opinion, according to the inclination of the person who adduces it. Gibbon has attacked with sarcasm and irony what has hitherto stood the test of reason and sound argument. Berrington, contrary to an opinion that has subsisted ever since the Reformation, endeavours to make Roman Catholicism palatable, and to reconcile its errors and abuses with justice, liberty, liberality: and afterwards Plowden closes the scene with an attempt to prove all establishments inconsistent with religion, while he recommends his own

as

SERMON VII.

[k] as readily coalescing with a particular party; from which what can follow but error, confusion, and every evil work. Alas, Christianity! since we see that the dissolution of the union, that naturally subsists between regular government and true religion, can only tend to destroy both; God's visible Church therefore must be materially injured; and, unless he had promised the contrary, be in the end totally extirpated by it. Our ardour, diligence, and perseverance in defending it, can only be excited by the prospects supplied by the idea of the invisible Church, to be represented now indeed only to the eye of faith, but which we know is founded on the purpose of God; which no power can change, no occurrences, human or divine, possibly prevent. This, under all circumstances, whether the face of the present world cheers or dismays, whether its events combine to vex, or even for the present to ruin us; whether we want or whether we abound, are established or only tolerated, privileged or unprivileged, slaves or free-born —this will still survive, and remain our unperishing consolation, our unfading glory, and inexhaustible source of joy.

[k] Appendix, ibidem, p. 583.

SERMON VIII.

Hebrews xi. 16.

For he hath prepared for them a city.

THE plan of these discourses approaches its termination; and what topic can better answer that purpose, than the consideration of that blessed and eternal state to which Christianity opens so bright and reviving a prospect, which is the really chief good of man, and which, connecting itself with the present scene, forms an whole at once complete and satisfactory, resolving every difficulty, and overcoming every possible objection. All surrounding objects, as well as the infirmity of our own frame, convince us of the perishing condition of this world: how absurd, then, to encourage hopes of permanent happiness here, when we have more reasonable grounds for the expectation of it hereafter! Our souls admit of improve-

improvement, and are impressed with desires more than necessary to, and beyond what can be satisfied in, a mortal state: there is therefore doubtless another arriving, in which our legitimate wishes shall be accomplished, and our aspiring nature will attain its designed perfection.

All estimation of ourselves, or of the world which we inhabit, will be incomplete, unless it is accompanied with considerations of the other; which surely are sufficiently important, nay glorious, to engage our most serious attention, did we not surmise that our sins and iniquities had deprived us of the power of supposing ourselves capable of them. Hence the pains of popular and licentious writers, as well the professed foes as the false and pretended friends of religion, to undermine and misrepresent those hopes as extravagant which they have spurned and rejected themselves; and, being exposed to the probability of misery, that others should expect to be eternally blessed, is more than they have patience to endure. Thus they deprive themselves, and those in the same wretched situation, of the only remaining remedy; namely, repentance and amendment of life. Nor is a future admittance into the heavenly city incompatible with the

SERMON VIII.

the comforts and conveniencies of this life, when innocent and suitable to our respective situations. However, the enjoyment of them must never interfere with our great and eternal reward, but must be always rendered subservient to the attainment of it. Virtue, learning, liberty, are the most eminent of earthly advantages; yet only so when they are acquired, practised, enjoyed under a sense of religion. Virtue, without the aid of Christianity, is a glaring unsubstantial meteor, neither permanently brilliant, nor in the event advantageous. Learning, too, without this its indispensable associate, far from profiting, is rendered highly prejudicial to society; and a love of liberty becomes mere licentiousness, unless such a privilege is considered as the gift of God, who may be supposed as well to approve of its rational enjoyment, as to discountenance its absurd and multiplied abuses.

If Priests, as it has been objected to them, have been all along in league with earthly governments for the subversion of freedom, their success has been very inconsiderable; in this respect the men of the world have been always an overmatch for the men of religion. As far as profane history is concerned, few Priests or none have rendered themselves conspicuous

spicuous as kings or conquerors: the Roman Catholic faith, indeed, has exemplified, in modern times, the power of religious prejudice, and of the monopoly of learning, to bend the human mind to the most abject slavery; but assertions with respect to that corrupted Church, cannot at all reach a pure and reformed religion.

In this state of probation to which we are at present subjected, it is likewise found that the most learned are not always the most virtuous; yet even they excite the diligence of others, though learned, yet religious, as well to qualify themselves for *answering those who ask them a reason for the faith that is in them*, as to counteract the designs of its enemies, and to refute, with equal pains to those employed on the contrary side, the objections that are continually brought against it. Not many wise, says the Apostle, are called; that the success of the Gospel might not be attributed to human counsel or contrivance, which are as often engaged on the side of vice as on that of virtue. Superior mental accomplishments are likewise too apt to produce pride and presumption; which, as they are far from congenial to the manners of the heavenly city, so they have been known to expel from a similar situation

SERMON VIII.

situation beings of a superior order to ourselves. Nor is learning necessarily connected with freedom. All human science arose like the sun in the east; yet those extensive regions, though under his rising beams, have never been cherished by them into freedom. The most famous and most copious libraries first appeared in Africa, under the Ptolemies, whose power was more absolute than we of this nation can possibly conceive. The golden age of Roman literature was likewise that of tyranny. So again, when an universal night had buried all arts and sciences, they revived, together with chemistry and medicine, among the Arabians, the confessed victims of Mahometan despotism; and modern Europe owes more, even in the arts, the mathematics, and in natural philosophy, to one nearly lawless monarch [1], than the whole world to all the republics that have ever existed.

And this is said with an intention of combating the now so common assertion, that to be free it is necessary that we should be illumined with greater, and perhaps different knowledge, than that which has hitherto appeared; or, in other words, that there has been from remotest ages a conspiracy existing of the learned against the illiterate, to oppress and enslave

[1] Lewis XIV.

enslave the latter; and that, were science universally disseminated, the bonds of this servitude would immediately be dissolved, and the whole human race would be regenerated, as it were, to truth, virtue, and liberty[m].

But we see the world around us exhibiting incontrovertible signs of decay. Those who have preceded us on this terrestrial theatre, at the longest have not remained long; and ourselves, by disorders, indispositions, and the failure of our faculties, are continually, as we advance, reminded that we are but strangers and pilgrims, that we must soon follow the appointed path trod by our predecessors, and make our exit also. As to letters too, how can a general inclination to them be excited among many, who seem neither disposed nor qualified for their attainment? It is only from a few being enabled to confine themselves to the pursuits of learning, that any progress at all can be made in its various branches. Were all to attempt it, they must soon relinquish the scheme, as their ordinary wants and necessities would interrupt and divert them from it. The most eminently accomplished likewise find in this earthly state, with what pains, and to how small a degree science is acquired, and how soon years and infirmities steal away the

[m] Vide Condorcet's Progress of the Human Mind, p. 62.

knowledge

knowledge which is derived from faculties, the extraordinary use and exercise of which too often impairs and destroys them; a sorrowful consideration indeed, did not reason, strengthened by revelation, thence infer the futility of relying upon any permanent advantages here, and derive from it a firm and certain hope, that the diligent use of our at present imperfect talents will prepare us for more valuable and infinitely higher degrees of knowledge hereafter; *for now we see through a glass darkly; but then shall we know, even as also we are known.*

[n] As then men do not, have not, nay cannot, under the present state of nature, proceed from virtue to learning, and from learning to liberty, why they do not can only be explained by the supposition of a better state subsequent to the present; and in this view our world, if not absolutely the best possible, yet is so perhaps, when considered relatively to the other. The division of mankind into the wise and ignorant, is not the effect of design; it is the necessary consequence of the present circumstances of their being: but they have arranged themselves into distinct classes; namely, the good and the bad. On this distinction

[n] Condorcet, p. 116.

religion builds her sanctions, which however she endeavours to soften, obviating, by the doctrine of repentance, the necessity of punishment, and comprehending, through her gracious promises, all within the circle of her glorious recompenses.

And who sees not, how incompatible with such a state, with such hopes and expectations of futurity, are those abstract ideas of perfection, that are now so commonly attributed to mankind? Were all equally virtuous or learned, no degree of liberty would be too much for them; their right to be considered as equals in this respect, would be unimpeachable; and all they could obtain by force (if force were necessary) would be justifiable on the grounds of reason: but under such a description the present world would be too good for them, and under their existing circumstances, for the glorious city, and that blessed state which Christianity teaches us to expect, it is to be feared they are at present not good enough. Their rights therefore must be circumscribed, their liberty in some degree abridged, and their natural privileges parted with, as they actually are, when the exercise of them is delegated to others, even at the very instant when they are owned and acknowledged.

In

In the actual state of man, his affections for terrestrial objects must be checked, and directed towards celestial. His passions must be controlled, not inflamed, and sources of comfort and consolation must be sought in humility and submission, not in pride and presumption; and all rules of conduct proposed to him must be regulated by this idea. All other plans of education, instruction, or legislation, however they may boast of being consonant to nature, will be found repugnant to his, as well as to that of the universe itself, of which he is a component part.

The existence of false religions affords no proof that all are false: a counterfeit is but a stronger argument of the reality of an original. False religions might conspire with the inventions of politicians, to effect merely state purposes; but Christianity could not, as it arose not from any sudden emergency; nor could any intermediate period be assigned for giving birth to it; but it was the effect of a continued scheme, successively carried on even from the fall of man to the present day. Had there been any interruption, inconsistency, or accommodation of it to any particular or private ends, it must have been discovered, by applying to general history, as well as to the series of prophecies to which it appeals in its support. Neither the Law, nor the Gospel in course succeeding it, intentionally admit of a popular and mysterious sense. It is true, that the records of them are contained in what are now called learned languages: but no one order of Priests, especially in the reformed Churches, understands more than another. Holy orders, if there is no impediment as to morality, are conferred on men of all ranks. If the Laity understand not as much as the Clergy, it is owing not to design, but merely to accident. We are ready to teach all we know to those that apply to us; and if any will be at the pains to surmount the difficulties of the same languages, there can be no objection to their acquiring as much of religious knowledge as ourselves: nay, as the fountains of divine Grace are alike open to all the members of Christ's mystical body, should that be afforded to any Layman in a larger proportion than to a Clergyman, he may possibly be thence enabled even to know more.

These suggestions are excited by the perusal of a literary work of a once celebrated French Essayist[p], intended to countenance and con-

---

[p] Condorcet on the Mind.

firm the new opinions, now, alas! too prevalent, and in disparagement of all religion whatever; in which he takes occasion to attribute to all Priests alike, from the very beginning, the same selfish designs against the welfare, comfort, and liberty of the rest of mankind, and taxes them with a similar and constantly preserved caution against trusting them with more knowledge than they could possibly help. The existence of the double doctrine, one for the initiated, another for the profane, he endeavours to prove from the Egyptian hieroglyphics; which he would represent as originally the invention of the sacred order, to answer that purpose. But they were intended to record events, or to communicate sentiments to all those that were capable of understanding them; they were therefore of the same use then, that alphabetic writing is of now. As well then might a man, totally devoid of education, affirm, that all that is written is the same mystery to others as it is to himself; as this author contends that all that is contained under hieroglyphics, was, at the time of its being represented by them, mystery, and known only to some particular persons, entrusted with the secret. The superiority that has been remarked, of alphabetic writing to hieroglyphics, is equally applicable to Christianity, when compared with a German mode of natural religion recently introduced [b]; since at this time of day all systems are accounted preferable to the revealed. Alphabetic writing, then, after it had been invented, was found so clear and convenient, that none, after once using it, could possibly have returned to the more intricate method of hieroglyphics; it must therefore have necessarily been as well subsequent as superior to it: so were we to quit the easy, natural, and readily occurring precepts of the Gospel, for that metaphysical religion, so abstracted and remote from vulgar apprehension, it were the same as to desert light for darkness, as, after having enjoyed the advantage of alphabetic writing, to resort to the clumsiness and obscurity of hieroglyphics.

‘Neither is the before-mentioned author more fortunate, in his assigning the origin of the double doctrine to the use of figurative terms in language, in the stead of the literal. For Priests have existed ever since the commencement of society; but figurative expression argues that it has been long established, and considerably improved: in this case,

[b] Professor Kant's.   [c] Condorcet, p. 62, 63.

SERMON VIII.

therefore, the effect would be prior to the cause. The truth is, that mythology is owing to a contrary cause; namely, to the too strict use of the literal, instead of the figurative meaning. To resolve its difficulty, recourse must be had, not to fancy, but memory; not the principles of painting, poetry, or metaphor; but analogy, definition, and etymology, must throw light upon the subject. This author, therefore, though the double doctrine certainly existed, yet has failed in assigning the causes of it, as well as in representing it for the purposes of mystery and despotism, as exclusively the invention of Priests.

[d] What absurdities may be expected from an author, who imagines the increase of science likely to extend the term of human life to antediluvian duration? This, could even the boasted virtue of the first ages be restored, would not exempt the human race from undergoing the certain fate which at last awaits them; a long delay of which would, in their present circumstances, only increase their misery, and detain them from that quiet and peaceful harbour, which, after a tedious and wearisome voyage, we must all wish to find.

[d] Vide Condorcet, p. 369.

Indeed, under the present circumstances of the world and of ourselves, nothing can be supposed more miserable, than that a man should be doomed to dwell here, oppressed with the inconvenient and distressing gift of immortality, especially when his situation was compared with the joys of that city which God has prepared for them that love him, *where they shall hunger no more, neither thirst any more, neither shall the sun light on them, nor any heat, but the Lamb that sitteth on the throne shall feed them, and lead them by living fountains of waters, and shall wipe away all tears from their eyes.*

Nor is this author more at variance with the common course of nature, than he is with himself.

ᵉ Notwithstanding his general charge against Priests of all descriptions almost throughout his works, as the abettors of deceit and tyranny; yet in one place he affirms, that their disputes amongst themselves tended to undeceive mankind, and to expose the weakness of those bonds in which they had been before enthralled. All therefore were not fast friends

Vide Condorcet, p. 108.

to arbitrary power, else they had remained more firmly united for the purpose of supporting and continuing it.

ᶠ Forgetful of his accusation of them in several passages, as generally hypocritical and vicious, in another place he represents them as disapproving of the unseemly conduct of some of their brethren, and appealing, in reproach of them, to the repositories of the common faith. Vicious conduct with vicious principles is infinitely less culpable than the same conduct with good—nay, if the principles are good, their intrinsic worth cannot be impaired by the occasional ill behaviour of those who embrace them; neither can *they* be represented as entirely depraved, who wish their own conduct, as well as that of others, to be judged by applying to it pure and pious principles.

ᵍ In one place he likewise declares, that it is according to nature that both sexes should be equally restrained by the marriage-contract, and, according to liberty, that either should dissolve the union, when it became burthensome or disagreeable. In ʰ another part of his

---

ᶠ Condorcet, p. 205. ᵍ Ibidem, p. 329, 356.
ʰ Ibidem, p. 20.

work.

work he traces the rife of fociety from the ties of family, which he fays is an impulfe of nature, indicated by the reciprocal affection of parents and their offspring continuing longer in the human than in any other fpecies, even after the purpofes of nourifhment and education have ceafed. Now this proceeds from him, who a little before had profeffed himfelf an advocate of fuch liberty and licentioufnefs, as rather makes it difficult to diftinguifh the father, and cannot produce much reverence to the mother. However, the laws made in confequence of fuch an extravagant opinion have been, or muft foon be repealed; a compliance with them having been found productive of extreme mifery. Conceit and Atheifm therefore, in this refpect, have been obliged to yield to the rational and decent precepts of revelation.

There never was a greater inftance than this author of the power of human learning to inflate, and, as it were, intoxicate the mind. Such attainments therefore are with great propriety very little regarded in Scripture, particularly when compared with virtue and righteoufnefs. It is to mathematical learning, it feems, and the modern difcoveries in natural philofophy, that all thefe fancied

cied advantages are owing. Now, not to dwell long on the enquiry, whether these studies are properly applied in searching after moral truth, this is certain, that no new tenets, however well founded, or seemingly ingenious, can possibly set aside what has been once established on the sure basis of indisputable fact, and the correspondent attestation of history. But this is a course of literature, which such authors, as the one at present considered, neither pursue themselves, nor recommend to others, unless through the medium of their own desultory and mangled compilations. However, if we would reap all the benefits to be expected from such a study, we must apply ourselves to the original; that is to say, to what are now called the learned languages. Indeed, no translation of works, professedly written on controverted subjects, is to be depended upon; nor can there be a greater sign of the degeneracy of the present age, than the low estimation in which it is now become the fashion to hold those real keys of erudition, from which have been derived almost all the arts and sciences that have illumined mankind, for a considerable portion of the period in which they have sojourned in this vale of sin and misery, conveying

veying down the stream of time the rich and copious stores of historic truth, and of political as well as of religious knowledge.

But the sufficiently versed in these languages will not only be enabled to confirm their faith, from the constant attestation afforded to it by the instructive page of history, but also further to increase it by the study, perhaps by the elucidation, of the antient prophecies, which still remain unfulfilled; which constitute a series of continued miracles, as it were occasionally to revive the zeal of succeeding Christians to the end of time.

How useful, then, would our progress be in the study of this still mysterious part of revelation, which yet directs us to look for and expect the establishment of the New Jerusalem, the city of our God, and of the Lamb, and which, as we are told, will be announced by signs predicted in prophecy, ere it actually takes place. And how will the expectation of, and thorough confidence in the reality of it, as well generally influence our moral conduct, as particularly inspire us with a desire of entering into that heavenly city, and strike us with apprehension lest we should be prohibited or excluded from it!

Such then are the advantages to be derived

SERMON VIII.

rived from the study of general history; and of which we of this place more especially have so eminent an opportunity of availing ourselves. Our Creator possessing infinite bliss and happiness, confined them not to himself, but communicated them to others; not merely to numberless people, but to infinite worlds. It is on this condition solely that objects inferior to him are distinguished by divine favours, otherwise they would be more ungrateful than the very inanimate parts of creation, many of which, *though having neither speech nor language, yet is their sound gone out into all lands, and their words, as it were, unto the ends of the world. How sweet then are the feet of those who bring the glad tidings of peace*, who lead men from the cares and anxieties of this wicked world, to that glorious and eternal city, *whose builder and founder is God*; who not only are employed in preparing legitimate inhabitants for it, but also in creating fresh joy to those already enrolled amongst its citizens, by recovering to hopes of admittance to it those once far gone, and lost in errors, vices, and crimes! Animated with such prospects ourselves, let us humanely and generously discover them to others; freely having received, let us freely give, and be proud of

the

the distinction of being fellow-labourers with Christ and with God. In our journey to the city which we profess to seek, let us be careful to engage as many associates as we can, and, if it be possible, *not to lose one*; to state all the motives we can to engage men to pursue it, and to remove every obstacle or impediment that may arise in their way thither. To contribute, though in a small degree, to so desirable a purpose, is the design of these Lectures; which alone, it is hoped, will excuse all the deficiencies in the execution.

FINIS.

A SERMON

PREACHED BEFORE THE

UNIVERSITY OF OXFORD,

On SUNDAY, October 18, 1795.

Hunc faltem accumulem donis, et fungar inani Munere.   Virgil.

John xi. 36.

Then said the Jews, Behold, how he loved him!

THIS was the reflection made by the spectators at seeing the tears of the blessed Jesus at the tomb of Lazarus, in whose family he was intimate, and with whom he had contracted a particular friendship; nay, whom by a miracle, as extraordinary as it was effectual, as a proof of his divine power, and to comply with the request of the sisters of the deceased, he raised from the dead after he had lain four days in the grave

Indeed, the Evangelist's account of our Saviour's grief on this occasion, comprised in two words only, seems to call our attention to it, and to discriminate it as a circumstance worthy of our serious consideration and repeated regard: *Jesus wept; Then said the Jews, Behold, how he loved him!* Yet that same Jesus was Lord of all things in heaven and in earth, equal to the Father as touching his Godhead. If then the indulgence of those affections, by which we so pleasingly cultivate

vate virtuous friendship while sojourning in this sublunary scene, was essentially wrong, surely he who was perfection itself had not been so distinguished for it; since he came into the world, that he might in all things leave us an example, that we might follow his steps: nay, if that fated journey, which we must all take, had been, circumstanced as we are, a blot or imperfection in the plan of Providence, and not on the whole conducive to our greater advantage, how easy for him, who was likewise Omnipotence itself, either at first never to have introduced it, or to have suppressed it afterwards, and thus not only to have removed all pain and grief, but also entirely to have done away their causes. But the Lord of life himself underwent that common calamity, and so reconciled us to it, by representing it as a passage to a better, and to an eternal existence: yet to confirm the utility, and avow the amiableness of sorrow for departed friends, he, who was the most perfect character ever known, was conspicuous for it, and on this occasion particularly shewed himself *a man of sorrows, and acquainted with grief.*

For sorrow viewed in a natural light, though never at first willingly admitted, yet in the end

end fails not to improve and relieve our nature. We should on many occasions be nearly hardened to stone, did not these softening drops abundantly flow; which, though they prove the weakness, yet are they at the same time an infallible sign of the amiableness of our disposition. In such situations likewise, the streaming eye naturally awakens the sympathy of others, which they in general, unless they are sadly debased and embruted, are ready enough to impart, but which the afflicted themselves, on another occasion, from the remembrance of their own sorrows, are strongly impelled to return; and thus may even grief itself be said to tend to the general advantage, as well of those who indulge, as of those who commiserate it.

Indeed as all passions, when carried to excess, are blameable, so sorrow, when extravagant, is no longer justifiable, not even by our Saviour's example, who in all things promoted our comfort, in none our absolute disquiet. For then sorrow becomes worldly, and the end of it is death; but when of a godly sort, it attains its best purposes, and worketh repentance to salvation, not to be repented of. It is certainly even good to be afflicted, when

a more

a more accurate observance of the divine statutes is the consequence. Did not the intervening hand of salutary chastisement thus check us in our career of vanity and dissipation, how closely attached should we be to this earth; how disinclined to, and disqualified for, that better state, which can alone satisfy the desires of an immortal soul! When amidst the constant decay and succession of earthly objects we see not merely the more advanced in years, but those who set out with us, nay those who are younger than ourselves, perhaps our acquaintance and friends, disappear, our sorrow, if it be at all effectual to our reformation, will not fail to remind us of the manifest brevity and incertitude of our present life. Whatever nature has of frail and transitory, the fading flower, the ephemeral insect, the momentary meteor, represent the similarly rapid caducity of man. What remedy then against the uncertainty and instability of the present scene, but to secure an interest in the more permanent and eternal! If reflection, which, but for the interference of sorrow, we had never known, engages us to do this, it has certainly been of infinite advantage to us, and has answered one of the purposes of our

God

God and Saviour, in implanting it in our breasts, and in himself becoming, as in the text, so eminent an example of it.

But when merit, talents, virtue die, how is our nature mortified, where otherwise there would be abundant matter for vanity and presumption! Yet here too sorrow, if rightly applied, would direct to useful reflexions, and lead from the contemplation of *their* excellencies, whose departure we deplore, to him, whom we should consider as the principal pattern, and original archetype of all perfection. If meekness, virtue, and amiableness are so attractive in man, how much more so must similar moral attributes be in him from whom man had his being, and who likewise impressed on his mind such commendable qualities! How could Epicurus say the universe was owing to chance; or the Stoics that it was animated by a soul of no more reason or sentiment than elementary fire? Can any thing give what it hath not? These rare instances then of human excellence are indisputable proofs of there existing somewhere benevolence ever exercised in our behalf, compassion ever inclined to relieve us, and power ever ready to protect us. The sensible heart, therefore, is affected at instances of baseness, ingratitude,

titude, hypocrisy; not merely as itself is concerned, but as they tend to weaken one species of evidence for the being of a God; while it reposes with pleasure and complacency on the consideration of such characters as were famous in their lives for science, virtue, religion; since they fill up the chasm that remained vacant in the proof of a presiding Providence, and tend to complete the otherwise apparently defective plan of creation, and to connect the present world with one infinitely better.

Yes, the possessed of merit, talents, virtue, die; yet *let us hope not eternally; for surely the care of them is with the Lord, and their reward is with the most High.* Nor indeed was it fitting that those emanations, as it were, of divine goodness should be long separated from the inexhaustible source of benevolence whence they sprung: as they were sent hither in some measure to reconcile us to our corrupted nature, so does their departure tend to confirm the hopes of its renovation and recovery. For were this the only sphere of their existence, why so short their abode here? But if they are removed to an happier residence, then it is surely well with them, and matter of consolation to us, to consider that where they are we shall

shall be likewise. Such lives, and such deaths, not only confirm the arguments struck out by the ingenious antients for the immortality of the soul, which before the discoveries of revelation were not entirely to be depended upon, but also strengthen and support the promises of Religion herself; for such characters we admire when living, and regret when dead. Now no innocent desire was ever implanted in vain; there is therefore reason to confide in Religion, when she assures us, that our admiration of extraordinary merit in those gone before us shall not be without its effect; that, if by patient *continuance in well doing we seek for it*, we shall be permitted to partake with them in happiness, where pure and sincere friendship shall not be again interrupted, but reciprocal love and affection shall know no end.

Such are the reflections suggested by religious sorrow; and where the characters that occasioned it were eminent and extraordinary, none that were acquainted with them can possibly be unconcerned: yet, as serious sentiments but occasionally prevail, it is the preacher's province, at least his apology, that, whenever they manifest themselves, he takes advantage of them for the purposes of moral improvement, of devotion, of piety. Thus the

the death of such men is rendered as instructive as their lives. All imputation of flattery is avoided, and their memory is recalled for ends to which the whole tenour of their actions was subservient, and to which, could they themselves be supposed sensible of what is passing, they would not be entirely averse.

What has been said, is intended to excite in your minds the recollection of [a] a great and extraordinary character (otherwise the introduction of him here had been somewhat improper), of whom the present year has deprived this place; one who, if any ever were, is surely worthy of being recorded as an example of singular merit, and of punctual performance of the respective duties of every station to which he was advanced.

Indeed what station could be unsuitable, what obligation burthensome, or what emergency oppressive, to him whom nature had endued with such strong and penetrating abilities? The most difficult subjects, the most perplexing questions, the most abstruse disquisitions, as if touched by the hand of magic, became easy and disentangled in his hands; a nice discrimination of character, and

---

[a] Dr. Dennis, the late President of St. John's College.

the happieſt conjecture as to probabilities, enabled him to predict ſuch events only as were ſure to come to paſs, and never to afford any advice which you afterwards repented of purſuing. His countenance was always marked with ſagacity, frequently animated with ſentiment and benevolence, and his manners were equally ſimple as ſincere. Being ſuch himſelf, an affected character was his abhorrence; perhaps he deteſted nothing more, except it were flattery. He was the laſt in the world to have ſaid, though many of high repute for underſtanding have ſolicited fame from others by the expreſſion, *orna me*—the world would not win him on any ſubject to ſpeak otherwiſe than he actually thought. He was naturally the meekeſt mortal living; yet his perſeverance and intrepidity, where he thought his duty concerned, were aſtoniſhing; otherwiſe he was gentle and placable, ſuppreſſing all animoſity in himſelf, and promoting peace and harmony among others.

This amiableneſs of diſpoſition, manifeſted during a whole life, produced him many friends, of whom he loſt none; for his counſel, his ſupport, his aſſiſtance, were always at the ſervice of thoſe who moſt wanted them. If he had any enemies, they did not long continue

tinue so; for they too were subdued by his impartial kindness and unremitted endeavours to do them good. His conversation was more than entertaining, it was delightful; as influenced by an heart eminently undisguised, liberal, and social. " I know," said he, " that " a man may seclude himself from, and at last " hate all mankind; but so will not I." None therefore that ever knew him, but prized his acquaintance, which none ever was obliged, through absence or avocations, to forego, but regretted it; for it was impossible to know him long without discovering that he was of the strictest integrity, the most unsullied honour, and of the purest principles, as well of religion as morality.

As a scholar too, his distinctions were eminent; and to me, at least, his knowledge appeared most valuable, because most practical. The Latin language, particularly the idioms, the very life and soul of it, he possessed *ad unguem*, as it is called. In these days, when reason, like virtue, seems in a great degree to have deserted us, as a logician he had few equals. No occasion ever saw him deficient in the more abstruse or recondite parts of science. Nay, as he was immensely distant from the parade so usual with smatterers, so were you

not

not unfrequently furprifed by his very extenfive acquaintance with the modern languages. His elegant mind likewife, at intervals, expatiated in the fields of tafte, and in the excurfions of refined amufement. In his youth he had not unfuccefsfully attempted poetry. Of mufic too and of painting he was no incompetent judge; accomplifhments which are highly ornamental, yet not abfolutely neceffary in thofe who may be fuppofed almoft wholly engroffed by fuperior ftudies and more important purfuits.

Nor, believe me, are thofe things foreign to the peculiar purpofes of this facred place; fince fuch employments and avocations have a moral, a religious tendency. The real fcholar can never be totally, or for a continuance corrupt. They who have fullied the purity of their minds amid fpeculations that might be fuppofed in a great degree to render them immaculate, have ufurped and violated the dignity of letters. No! accuracy of judgment, vividnefs of fancy, a delicacy of perception as to the finer objects of fenfe, are feldom partially exercifed, but have a general influence both on theory and practice, and diftinguifh as well the extraordinary genius as the good man; the elevation of whofe ftudies,

and

and even the elegance of his amusements, keep him at an infinite distance from every idea of vice or sin, of debasement or defilement.

But with respect to this extraordinary person, what words can do justice to his conduct as a governor of a society, which from the first to the last was directed by inflexible justice, and the most unimpeached impartiality? No irregularity could point at him as its pattern; no immorality could plead him as its excuse. Discipline too, in his reluctant hand, was not the instrument of pique or caprice; but you saw it was intended merely for the correction and reformation of the offender. That firm resolution, that adamantine integrity, that not the falling universe could otherwise shake, to the waywardness and petulancy of youth was patient, to an extraordinary degree indulgent, nay, even submissive. The satisfaction that he might have insisted on in public, he has been often known only not to court by the interference of common friends; nay sometimes condescended, for that purpose, to employ even personal remonstrance. The dawnings of genius too he was not only generous, but lavish, in forwarding: in short, he brought the society into that state, that it was good for it that he governed it while he did,

and

and unpropitious that he was so soon called away from it. That this was the general sentiment, the universal grief shewn at his death abundantly proved; and the tears which every eye, almost without exception, shed at his funeral: so that if a strict regard to his own duty, and an unremitted observance that others performed theirs; if to temper dignity with affability, and to connect authority with affection, speak the good governor, he was indisputably one.

That elevated and dignified manner accompanied him likewise into office as Vice-Chancellor. Though naturally fond of ease and retirement, yet, conscious how much opinions and practices prevailing here influence the kingdom at large, he was resolved that no dangers or difficulties should deter him from exerting his abilities for the honour and advantage of this place; and surely if success is a proof of propriety, his must be most unequivocal, through whom not only the University, at the Royal visit, ingratiated itself with the Sovereign, but such strong impressions were received of the particular personal merit of the presiding Magistrate, as were never afterwards, if report is to be depended upon, erased. When rumours of tumults and expected disorders prevailed in our streets, his manly mind was not abashed at them, but was prepared to meet them, and would doubtless have applied suitable and effectual remedies against them; so that the storm that threatened the very existence of the University was dissipated, and blew over merely through the prudence and vigilance of the Chief Magistrate, which they who caused these alarms did not choose to put to the trial: his known firmness and intrepidity awed them into peace.

And now, it may be asked, was this eminent and extraordinary character shaded with no failings? Yet is it somewhat unreasonable that, as an human being, he should be expected to have none. Fewer, perhaps, he had been supposed to have had, were the motives of his conduct, in all instances, better understood, and the general amiableness of his disposition more extensively known; for whatever might be the result of his actions, his intentions were always right. Perhaps too we may allow him that fault of active and superior minds, the not bearing with sufficient patience the slowness and infirmities of those whose thoughts are not quite so rapid, nor ideas so accurate, as their own. However, if you recollect that man among men, and it is

to

to be presumed, with God, is to be judged of, not from his absolute want of failings, but from the preponderancy of his good over his bad qualities; that likewise he for many years struggled with a radical and inveterate disease (for to that, and that alone, and not to any mental disquiet, his dissolution was owing); that, lest he should afflict his friends, relations, family, he for a long time presented hope in his countenance, while inwardly he was convinced that his case was absolutely desperate, and that the best men, under such circumstances, must have some allowances made for them; when all these things are considered, though in a solitary instance or two you may condemn, yet, on the whole, you will not be able not to approve, admire, and lament him.

It remains to speak of him as a Christian; a topic not obvious, because much of the excellence of that character depends on its being confined to privacy and retirement; yet if forgiveness of injuries, if compassion for the distressed, if an hand ever ready to relieve them, speak the Christian, he was unquestionably such. Sacred subjects formed not always the matter of his conversation: he could occasionally digress, from severe to gay,

from

from the inftructive to the merely entertaining; but though religion employed not conftantly his tongue, yet it was never abfent from his heart. The Chapel bell called not more conftantly to prayers, than he attended them. Many occurrences in his life fhewed, that, according to the advice of the antient philofophers, particularly of Pythagoras, he at night brought himfelf to account for the actions of the preceding day; and then, if it appeared that, through hafte, or inadvertency, he had offended any, however inferior, he refted not till he had made them fatisfaction. Before the celebration of the facrament, how careful was the good man to do away all, even the leaft furmifes of enmity betwixt himfelf and thofe who were to communicate with him in thofe holy myfteries. The preceding night faw all differences compofed, all matters of difcipline, however minute, fettled and concluded, that he might approach the altar in the words of David; *An offering of a pure heart will I make thee; be thou my witnefs, O Lord my God.* At laft the attentions, he had all his life long paid to religion, were returned to him, when they were moft neceffary; and he was enabled to give the ultimate, yet ftrongeft teftimony of the
fincerity

sincerity of his faith, by reflecting on his approaching fate with the utmost compofure and refignation: for in the bofom of the fociety he adorned, of the family he loved, and in the midft of the offices of the religion he had fo confiftently and ftrenuoufly profeffed, to his infinite advantage certainly, but to our inexpreffible lofs, he expired.

Then was feparated from its frail and mortal body, the foul of one of the beft of men, the beft of hufbands, the beft of fathers, and, alas! the beft of friends. Yet why, when there is that within that far furpaffeth *show*, this feeming pomp and parade, as it were, of grief?—Becaufe, though the partial hand may fomewhat overcharge the portrait, and the inexpert one fail of doing juftice to it, yet it were better fo done than not at all. Neither was it fitting that lineaments fhould pafs away unnoticed, from which may be copied the ftrongeft expreffions of amiablenefs, of fcience, of friendfhip, of piety. Befides, as to ordinary characters, oblivion cafts its undiftinguifhing veil alike over their death as over their life: but when the common fate involves the extraordinary inftances of human excellence, the mind recoils on itfelf, and, for a time at leaft, reflects on what it is, what it may be, and is

then

then most effectually persuaded to become what it ought to be. If any have experienced a similar loss, it were but charity to direct to the only remaining source of comfort and consolation, the hopes of the Gospel, and the promises of revelation. What an additional motive to continue in the accurate practice of Christian obedience, to reflect that it is the only probable means, the only rational foundation for the hopes of rejoining, in a better state, those once the objects of our affections here, who realized in their own persons all that we conceive of fair, of just, of good; who were sent but to be recalled, and loved but to be lamented! On the present subject I could willingly exhaust whole days, whole nights; but to prevent your fatigue, let us hasten to a conclusion. The variety of circumstances, the enmity of enemies, the frowns of fortune, were hitherto contemned and disregarded, till I lost thee, dearest friend; she then convinced me of her power in earthly affairs, and how much myself, in particular, was exposed to her shafts. There was then nothing more to be done, than to raise my supplicating hands, and intreat for mercy; yet still the stores of philosophy, and the comforts of religion, are near, as a support against every species of mischief

or

or misfortune. Nay, convinced as I am that thou art removed to a far happier place, the wish to recall thee were selfish and injurious: but if the amiable, excellent, long observed, and admired qualities of thy life shall be faithfully transcribed, as far as our respective stations will allow, into my own, our connexion will then have been advantageous indeed. For while memory indelibly retains them, thou mayest be still considered as regarding, as usual, and inviting me to renew thy sweet society, thy conciliating conversation; and then our meeting again may be the happier, from our present separation having been so displeasing—distressing—dejecting.

[b] Vide Cic. Consolationem, in fine. Tu vero, quando me insigni et excellenti tuarum laude, memoriâque virtutum, tam præclare juvisti, nunc ab hominibus sejunctus, non me deserens, sed aliquando respectans, perduc eo, ubi tua tandem collocutione conspectuque fruar; ut et parenti tui amantissimo, quam potissimum optare debes, gratiam referas, et ego multo mihi gratiorem multoque jucundiorem congressum nostrum futurum intelligam, quam insuavis et acerbus digressus fuit.

THE END.

ERRATA.

P. 16. l. 5. for *the* read *thy*
18. l. 7. after *follow* dele the *semicolon*
39. l. 5. for *in* read *by*
58. l. 13. for *admire* read *admit*
64. l. 16. after *mean* insert *for it*
74. l. 15. for *exist* read *exists*
82. l. 7. after *or* insert *of*
95. l. last, for *allowing* read *allowing*
110. l. 11. for *they* read *it*
115. remove the reference ¹ from *the* in the first line to *licence* in the seventh
117. l. 6. insert a full point at *Catholics*
—— l. 7. after *time* dele the *colon*
126. remove the reference ⁵ from *even* in the thirteenth line to *our author* in the nineteenth
128. remove the reference ᵘ from *successor* in the second line to *ally* in the fourth
132. l. 27. after *ambition* dele —
149. l. last, for *are* read *is*

www.ingramcontent.com/pod-product-compliance
Lightning Source LLC
Chambersburg PA
CBHW021732220426
43662CB00008B/815